The Strength of Our Anchors

Presented by: Dawn Bornheimer

Book cover photo credit: Loro Borromeo D'Agostino

Published by Write the Book Now, an imprint of Perfect Time SHP LLC.

ISBN: 9781732989535

Dedication

"I dedicate this book to my eight-year-old self. I see you, I love you, and you are enough."

Table of Contents

Introduction

"A day will come when the story inside you will want to breathe on its own. That's when you'll start writing."

-Sarah Noffke

There is power in sharing your story, whether you are standing in front of a room full of people, sitting across the table from a friend, sharing it in a blog post, posting a video on social media or writing it down for others to read. Stories are a way of sharing things about ourselves to build authentic connections, giving us a chance to see the humanness in one another. Some of us are more willing than others to be vulnerable, often this goes back to an earlier time when we took a chance and shared a part of ourselves with someone. If what we shared was met with blame, shame, anger, disappointment, or judgment, we learned at that moment that sharing part of us was not safe. We carry that feeling forward along with what we made it "mean about us", with us into our adult life. It is only when we are willing to unpack those early memories and moments, that we can choose to redefine them.

Christian musician, Morgan Harper Nichols, encourages us to "tell the story of the mountain you climbed. Your words could become a page in someone else's survival guide." We have to decide how we want to show up for ourselves and others each day while releasing ourselves and others from the past. This will allow us to co-create a beautiful tomorrow.

Since the beginning of time, we have been sharing stories to warn, to inspire action, to guide, or to connect. Stories bind us together to make sense of the world and they allow us to share that understanding with others. As an elementary school teacher, I would often read books to my students, stories about other kids their age, helping them to learn more about compassion, friendship, patience, kindness, and other soft skills. Textbooks used both fiction and non-fiction stories to set the stage for the lesson in one of the various subjects we would teach. We have all been captivated by a movie or book, the peek into someone else's world or life experience while welcoming the escape from our own.

I invite you to think about stories a little differently as you continue on with this book. *The Strength of Our Anchors* contains the personal stories from nine beautifully unique individuals who like all of us, have a story to tell. One of the most remarkable things for me as I have connected with each of these women is their willingness to surrender to the pen (or keyboard), to be just a little more vulnerable than is comfortable, and allow the story to flow through them. It is so powerful to move through your story, to identify the tools you now have in your toolbox of life, and to know you don't have to STAY in your story. It is my hope that you will see glimpses of yourself in their words or simply have a greater sense of compassion for one another as many of these women suffered in silence at some point.

Like so many others who are navigating this thing called life, these women have experienced illness, fear, grief, overwhelm, depression, divorce, tears, isolation, and disconnect. These same women found themselves through community and connection, compassion, fitness, coping strategies, joy, support, faith, and gratitude. Lisa Nichols, New York Times Best Selling Author and Transformational Speaker, suggests that when we "swing open the closet doors' and learn to love the darkest parts of ourselves, we will have "Nothing to Prove, Nothing to Hide, Nothing to Protect, and Nothing to Defend".

In preparation for sharing my own story, *Shifting My Identity*, as part of an anthology in the Spring of 2018, I began listening to TED Talks, reading books, listening to podcasts, and journaling. During this time, now affectionately known as the excavation process, I came across a TED Talk by Najwa Zebian. Her message was so powerful, it moved me to tears as I connected with her pain and passion, her vulnerability and pure heart. At that moment, I said to myself, "I wish I could hug her and tell her, I experienced something similar and thank her for naming it. As the universe would have it, my vision came true, in October 2018 I had the pleasure of meeting Najwa

Zebian, author, speaker, and educator at The Summit of Greatness in Columbus, OH.

When I saw she was going to be one of the speakers, I knew I was meant to be there. Just as I imagined, she was fantastic on stage, a perfect balance of vulnerability and transparency while being soft-spoken, and genuine. Her pure heart radiated throughout the theater, she felt so held in those moments as the audience was fully engaged in her message. Najwa Zebian, without knowing it, has been a mentor to me with her message and the strength she has demonstrated, the words she has chosen, and the example she has set through her own actions. I waited in line after she spoke to hug her, to have her sign my book, and to thank her for her vulnerability because she allowed me to name the hurt I had once felt and I wanted her to know I was happy, I was living a beautiful life, and that self-love is not selfish. If each of us can reach at least one person, if we can gift someone with the knowledge that they are not alone, and in the process allow our own story to breathe, then we can give others permission to share their own stories when they're ready.

Below is a powerful poem from one of Najwa Zebian's self published book, *Mind Platter.*

"Just One Choice" -

Everyday life will give you many things to choose from. You can choose to remain in your state. Or to change it. You can choose to dwell on the past. Or to move forward toward the future. You can choose to believe in yourself. Or to be hard on yourself. You can choose to ask for more. Or to be grateful for what you have. And you don't have to decide on everything every single day. But at least make one choice. Take the lead in your life by choosing instead of giving into helplessness. With time, choice becomes a habit. If you don't know what to choose today, here is a choice that you can never go wrong with: gratitude. Be grateful for what you have, even if you feel that you deserve more. If you are not thankful for what you already have, there is no guarantee that you will be grateful with more.

As you begin reading the following contributions, please do so with an open heart. Please know that each of these women has taken a great risk in being vulnerable, some sharing things in this book that they have never said out loud. They have embraced vulnerability in the hopes of reaching at least one person by sharing their stories. It takes courage to share parts of yourself but when we acknowledge that sharing our stories is bigger than us, when we are willing to see the lessons in some of our darkest moments, we emerge stronger than we could have imagined.

"When you come out of the storm, you won't be the same person who walked in. That's what this storm's all about. "
-Haruki Murakami

PRESENTED BY: DAWN BORNHEIMER

Erin Antroinen

"The true warrior isn't immune to fear. She fights in spite of it." --
Francesca Lia Block

Finding the Warrior Within

By: Erin Antroinen

Have you ever felt like you were at the top of your game? Like really at the top of your game, personally, professionally, relationally, spiritually. Well that was me in 2015/2016. I was running the young adult ministry at my church, I had just rebuilt my health and life after three car accidents in five years, I had a beautiful home, a thriving business that I had established myself, my team in the top 1200 out of 1.1 million, and I became a nationally ranked powerlifter that year in the 100 percent raw division in my age bracket….life was good. I felt like I was firing on all cylinders and was unstoppable. Little did I know my life was about to change dramatically.

For a few months leading up to July 2017, I felt like I was forgetting things more frequently, I was becoming more absent-minded and my energy levels were declining, but I did what every "strong" entrepreneur does, I pushed through and kept going. Ministry meetings and events, leading my top team in my company, powerlifting training four days a week, and attempting to have a social life with family and dating until one day my whole world stopped.

I was at my companies yearly seminar and flying high

after having an incredible year. I was walking in the middle of a huge corridor with people everywhere...I began to feel flush and clammy on the back of my neck and hands like I was going to pass out...my eyes filled up with tears, I couldn't get control of my mind or body. The entire room was spinning and I was unable to focus on anything as I got low in my skirt suit and began to crawl my way from the middle of the corridor to the side of the walkway to a wall. I was going through the checklist in my head..."did I get rest, have I drank water, did I eat today?" The answer was a resounding YES, "then what could it be?" The women around me began to ask me how they could help and who could they call, I couldn't stand or walk, speak or even remember my friends' names "what was happening to me????" All I could do was pray.

For the last three days of the seminar, I was unable to even walk without someone holding me up on either side like an injured football player getting escorted off the field. I tried just about any over the counter medication that treated vertigo, dizziness, or motion sickness and nothing worked. Upon arriving home the journey of finding out what was happening began. We tried EVERYTHING in an attempt to diagnose what was going on with me. Initially, I visited my general practitioner, chiropractors, cranial therapist, acupuncture specialist, a few visits to the Emergency Room, as well as an ear, nose, and throat specialist. I went through a battery of tests by everyone to include CT scans and X-Rays as well as both long and heavy doses of numerous antibiotics and antihistamines. All of this did not get me any closer to an answer to what was going on with me. In my new reality with my entire body rebelling against me I knew that the one thing that I could control was my attitude. Over the next 90 days while I was being tested it was a daily battle to choose joy. So I made positive affirmations about being healthy, being happy, and thriving in the storm, added scripture to them and each day I faced the uncertainty of what life was dishing out with a smile, even if some days it was forced.

After nothing was working my doctor decided it was time to pull out the big guns, a full neurological workup; head contrast MRI and series of tests in a neurological study clinic. We waited for what felt like months, but in reality was a week only to hear my neurologist utter the words, "everything looks normal."

WHAT! As I sat there I felt so conflicted, relieved that it wasn't anything diagnosable major, but feeling terrified because if none of this tells me what is wrong with me...what do I do? The neurologist's plan was heavy doses of steroids and migraine medicine to "see if it worked." He had no official diagnosis, No treatment plan.

Life was miserable, I was desperate, and knew in that moment there had to be another option! I was willing to do or try ANYTHING to get some relief. My girlfriend got me in to see her holistic specialist. I had my first couple of assessments. We discovered that my body was toxic with heavy metals, chemicals, Sucralose, and mycotoxin black mold that I had somehow come in contact with which are all toxic to the proper functioning and health of my brain and nervous system. It was the perfect storm of toxicity in my body to mimic MS and other severe neurological conditions, but prayerfully with time, holistic treatments, and physical therapy I would get my life back. I thought the following months were merely going to be a physical health journey to detox and create a new healthy body but little did I know my entire life was going to be transformed and this was the first step in a longer journey.

Over the following months getting my health back was my focus so everything in my life took a 180-degree turn and shifted. I stepped down from leading the ministry at my church, my business dropped significantly, I wasn't able to complete any of my powerlifting training, and to top it all off I had to move out of my home over the Christmas holidays. I had to get rid of almost everything I owned because the mold spores had invaded it and the risk of contamination was too high to try to keep it. My life was being turned upside down, but even as I was watching all my belongings literally being thrown away I was humbled by God's grace in providing for me a loving home to live in while I healed. A safe haven that I could get the help I needed, a place that I could truly not worry and begin healing not only my physical body but the spiritual and mental parts of me that today are the foundations of who I authentically am.

Shortly after I moved, I remember so vividly sitting in my holistic treatment crying. Even though I was so grateful I couldn't shake the feeling of losing everything that I thought made me, me. Every title I had, every belonging I owned, every shred of my self-dignity...I was at the bottom with no site of getting out of this. In this moment my Holistic practitioner walks in, recommending I use a cane so I can get out and continue the journey of healing and health. Everything in me screamed...it has been six months into this journey and I am still being driven and escorted everywhere. Why was this happening to me? The woman who works to be the BEST at everything I do... not only do I need to be driven around but now you want me to use a walking device at the age of 33?! As I laid there I continued to have a mini adult tantrum. I was mad at God...I work so hard to be great at everything I do, I couldn't understand, what have I done to deserve this? At this very moment, my girlfriend texted me a scripture that changed my perspective and I believe was a pivotal turning point in my journey....Mark 6:8 NLT - "He told them to take nothing for their journey except a walking stick--no food, no traveler's bag, no money." It was in this moment I didn't know how but I knew God was going to see me through this. I was bone weary but I needed to grab onto the little bit of faith I had left and just take the next best step. In this moment I knew I was being called to surrender IT ALL and one lesson I had learned before was delayed obedience is still disobedience. So, I got a cane.

I began asking myself questions like, who am I? What do I really want in life? How will I get through this? My raw truth was, I didn't know. I had spent most of my life as an adult being run by the phrase, "fake it til you make it" to give me the confidence to become the person I truly wanted to be. But, somewhere I interpreted that phrase as pretend to be who you think you need to be in order to accomplish all your dreams, it was as if I lived a double life. Being sick made me wake up and see that I am running a business where I mentor women to become the best version of themselves and the reality was that I had "faked" it so much I didn't even know my own truth. I made the decision in this moment to use this season of separation as preparation for what will be the next best chapter of my life.

There is an African proverb that reads..."When **there is no enemy within**, the **enemy** outside can do you **no** harm." I have learned that in order to step into the best version of me I needed to stop pretending. The truth is I was undisciplined but could make myself "look" super busy" and successful. The truth is I felt unworthy to be loved because of an abusive relationship that for years I continued to feel less than capable in my relationships and work and as a result, I overcompensated and kept people at a distance to hide my unworthiness. The truth is I didn't think I deserved success because I had an abortion years ago and who am I to get God's best when I couldn't be trusted with another life. I agreed with the man I was seeing at the time for the procedure, even though in my heart I knew it was wrong. Through the abusive relationship, the abortion, and NOW this illness I was allowing the things people did to me, the decisions people made for me, and the illnesses that just happened to me to rob me of my future. It was in the season of losing my child by my own decisions that I gave my life to Christ and learned my REAL truth, that I am fearfully and wonderfully made and so are you. No matter what has happened to you or what decision you have made God loves you and you are never too far away for Him to welcome you back home. When we choose to look at all the things in our life through a lens of grace we realize we no longer need to fight the person within, peace is restored and joy can be found even amidst the most turbulent times.

Once I truly owned who I was, the good, bad and the ugly I had to embrace the process or the suck as I like to call it. The day in, day out, daily, hour by hour, and in the beginning minute by minute process of accepting who I am, including every decision I have ever made and stepping into who God is calling me to be. But the funny part is that most times it takes a while for your outside world to catch up with the vision you see on the inside. I wrote the vision out of who I would be, what my health looked like, what my future relationship with my husband would be like, what my multi-million dollar business would be and how it would run, I made sure to get as specific as possible with every area of my life and who I wanted to be when there was no evidence of ANY of these things happening in my life. And each day I went after it. Just me. My mirror. My God. No recognition and no applause. Each day I prayed like it was up to God and worked like it was up to me. Even though God blessed me with an incredible tribe of people to walk through this with, this inner work was up to me. If I was going to step into the next that God had for me it was imperative that I shifted my faith, beliefs, and mindsets and even though I didn't see it yet these were perfect conditions for growth.

Overcoming an illness, creating an abundance mindset and business systems, and while overcoming limiting beliefs can be hard, but so is staying sick, working too hard, negative thinking, and being broke. Choose your hard! I wish I could tell you every day was a little bit better than the last, but more often than not I felt mentally or physically that I would take one step forward and ten steps back. I had to master the art of progress over perfection and learn how to celebrate small wins because small wins compounded over time would lead to big victories. I learned very quickly to manage the day to day emotions and to find joy in the journey not in only what I was accomplishing, but in who I was becoming. Each morning I would write the five things I was most grateful for, my top three things I was working to accomplish, and my top three habits that supported those things. Every night I would journal those moments that seem like a coincidence but I like to call them God winks. You will recognize them as your daily intentions and effort colliding seamlessly with your reality to be reminded that God is in the details. I also wrote out three to five things I was most proud of myself for that day AND three to five things I forgave myself for. This may seem silly, but it is the seemingly insignificant details of what we do in our daily routines that make all the difference in whether we overcome that thing to step into God's best for our life.

Progress isn't pretty, we miss the mark sometimes, but if we are aware of what we are grateful for, can celebrate the small wins daily, and then acknowledge where we are falling short and forgive ourselves we unconsciously give ourselves permission to be our BEST each and every day. The expectation no longer is perfection, but a standard of excellence that allows grace to shape us into the best version of ourselves no matter what trial or tribulation you are currently walking through. Our greatest point of pain then becomes our greatest ability to impact others when we choose to face it, consciously walk through it, and find the warrior within.

PRESENTED BY: DAWN BORNHEIMER

Gratitude and Acknowledgements from the author:

<u>Erin Antroinen</u>

Mom and Dad (Sue and Jeff Antroinen)

Sister Megan Antroinen

Nephew Josh Antroinen

Extended family

Mike and Tina Hilson and Family

Kim and Jason Williams

Camarie and Jeremiah Vedis

Dee Kline and Staff family

John Flagg

Denice Williams

Kelly Shurgot

Naomi Wethje

Jennifer and Ashraf Faramawi

Michelle Boyce

Chris Daniel RIP

Pam and Joe Higgs

Shannon Gragg

Emily Watts

Sarah Miller

Leah Woodard

Sarah Foster

Therese Simon

Carolyn Fortney

Lara Fortney-McKeever

Quentin Caboga

Justin and Jennifer Bagley

New Life Church & Staff

My Mary Kay Sisters

My Customers

My Team

The Barbellas

301 Strong Family

Catherine Foundation and Staff

About Erin Antroinen

At the early age of 20, Erin began her business as a skin care and beauty influencer with Mary Kay cosmetics, while going to school to be a pharmacist. Erin quickly found her love for entrepreneurship and 6 months after starting her business took the leap of faith to pursue it full time. Only a short 6 months later Erin quickly moved up the ranks to the top 1% of the company as an Independent Sales Director earning the exclusive pink Cadillac. I'd say she found her nitch! Fourteen years later, Erin continues to build her business leading an incredible team of Warriors around the country.

Erin specializes in leadership development, growing relationships, and helping women to build the warrior within. She shows women how they can run a side hustle or create a full-time business to create time/financial freedom from the corporate workplace to live their dream life. This year Erin will become Innermetrix certified, a diverse personality assessment that will help individuals/teams to identify who they are, what motivates them, and how to leverage decision making to own the warrior within, to make an impact in the world. Connect with Erin via Facebook, Instagram, and LinkedIn.

Jackie MacDougall

So much has been given to me; I have no time to ponder over that which has been denied. -- Helen Keller

IT'S BEEN A WONDERFUL LIFE

By

Jackie MacDougall

I could barely hear the genetic counselor over the screams of my four-week-old baby. Like most days, he was wailing at the top of his lungs and we were at a loss how to please him.

What do you want? I'll do anything.

It's not like we hadn't just had a baby boy 16 months before him. But this was different. Every morning, I woke up thinking today would be the day that he'd feel better, that he'd be happy. I changed my diet to help make my breast milk easier on his tummy. My husband and I created a foolproof system to tag team our 11-pound shrieking newborn so neither of us would run away, never to return. We were exhausted, frustrated and wondering what the heck we had just done.

As I stood in the small, private office bouncing my screaming boy in my arms, the counselor informed me it would be at least a month before we'd receive the results. I was finally going to find out if I carried the same genetic mutation that ultimately killed my 39-year-old mother, taking her away from her husband and 11 kids. I was the youngest at just three years old.

I don't remember my mother having cancer. I don't even remember when she died. I only remember growing up feeling like a part of me was gone, knowing how lost I felt but having no recollection of the series of events that led to it. I was surrounded by siblings who, how it appeared to me anyway, felt the loss of the actual woman they remembered, not just an *idea* of what she represented.

What did her voice sound like?

Am I like her?

Did she laugh like me?

Like grief has a funny way of doing, I was hit over the head with the loss off and on during my childhood, often during what felt like the most inconvenient times of my life and when I was *supposed* to be at my happiest.

But I wasn't. I was just sad and confused -- lost. How could I miss someone so damn much that I couldn't even remember? The inner critical judgment of my feelings only made things worse. *Why are we as humans often hardest on ourselves during the times we need the most support?* As I pushed my way through the awkward teen years and into young adulthood, I became increasingly impulsive, sometimes even reckless. I processed my feelings through alcohol, toxic relationships and some seriously questionable choices. Let's just send a big thank you to the universe that social media didn't exist during my decades-long phase of self-exploration.

I remember the first time I heard about the genetic link to my mother's cancer, a mutation called BRCA1. It was the early 2000s and I was on the phone with my sister, listening to her educate me while I paced around my small southern California home. It's not like we hadn't suspected a genetic connection sooner, given that two of my mother's four sisters had also died of cancer. We also had cousins who had been diagnosed and gone through treatment. My sister described how she, along with my other sisters, had been tested for the mutation. But unlike my other sisters, she did test positive. The words that followed were like something you'd hear from one of Charlie Brown's incoherent teachers. All I really got out of it was that she would likely undergo preventative surgeries and have both breasts removed, as well as her ovaries.

Is she insane? Why would she do that? A genetic mutation is not a diagnosis! What. Is. She. THINKING?

It was 2003. I had been married less than a year. We were starting to think about babies. I couldn't even imagine being tested, never mind make a decision to drastically change my body forever.

I wasn't the most understanding sister in that moment. If I have any regrets, that is one of them. My sister is 14 years older than I am and experienced our mother's death much differently from my three-year-old self. She needed to make decisions based on what she felt she needed to do for herself, her husband, and her five kids. She was a warrior and I couldn't even see it.

Until I could.

So here I am on that fateful day in late 2005, standing in the genetic counselor's office, rocking my screaming child back and forth, finally ready to get the information that could change my life. I was married and had given birth to my two baby boys, I knew it was time for me to find out if I had the mutation. I was 34 years old, just five years younger than my mom when she died. Once I heard that cancer can take years to develop, I knew it was important for me to know what I was up against.

December 5, 2005

Several weeks after that appointment, I was home rocking my baby in a La-Z-Boy recliner while watching my toddler play on the floor next to me. My husband had just run down to the local grocery store to pick up some necessary items before he was to head off to a long night of video editing. The phone next to me rang and I picked it up.

Hi.

Uh-huh.

Okay.

I understand.

I hung up the phone. I felt like someone had just poked me with a stun gun. Holy shit. I carried the BRCA1 mutation. I kept rocking my son, my head spinning yet my body paralyzed with fear. A few minutes later, my husband walks in, his arms filled with groceries.

I kept rocking.

He puts the groceries away, none the wiser that I had just received a call that would change the course of our lives. I wanted so badly to tell him, to fall into his arms in a ball of emotions. But no. I know my husband. He would've called in sick to work to stay home and take care of me. Anyone in TV knows that a freelancer calling in sick last minute is the kiss of death. He was working on a project with an intense schedule and was killing himself already to finish the work required to enjoy two paid weeks off at the end of the year. This was not the time to distract him with emotional news. So I stayed quiet. I sat in silence, rocking back and forth, wondering what I was going to do. When Jeff returned home sometime in the middle of the night, I sat up in bed.

I have the gene.

I lay back down, still feeling numb, and he curled up behind me. I don't know how long we lay there silently before we dozed off, only to be awaked a few hours later by the sound of the baby.

The days that followed that phone call felt like a blur. I began to research everything I could about the risks, talked to women —including my sister— who had been-there-done-that and made appointments with some of the top doctors in the LA area. I was determined to take on this challenge with a clear head and a logical plan of attack. There was no room for emotion, I told myself. I've got work to do.

As my husband approached his time off at work, I couldn't wait to have him around for two whole weeks. And the fact that they'd be paid (that's like finding a unicorn in the freelance TV world), I felt like we were being sent a gift from above. Finally, someone understood what we needed and was providing.

Until my husband walked in early one night from work.

I was laid off.

And we're losing our insurance.

They found a lump. Could I come in the following day to discuss next steps? Uh, yeah.

During that appointment, I'd receive the contact information for a breast surgeon, something I was already considering as a preventative step but this certainly changed things.

I met the surgeon, a quirky yet confident doctor who both scared the crap out of me and calmed my nerves — simultaneously. She shared that I wasn't a candidate for a needle biopsy as the lump was positioned in a way they couldn't reach. Instead, it would require a surgical biopsy. Given the level of research, I had done over the past two months, I knew a surgical biopsy would be invasive and, if they did discover I have cancer, with the increased risk of it returning multiple times due to my BRCA status, it would ultimately lead me to a bilateral mastectomy. I looked at my husband and we both knew what needed to happen next without even saying a word to each other.

Just take 'em.

I was wheeled into surgery March 16th, 2006, a decision I have never regretted, not even when I woke up to the news several hours later that I did not have cancer. And I certainly didn't regret it when my surgeon revealed four days later that pathology had shown pre-cancer growing in the other breast. "You dodged a bullet, young lady," she said while standing at the end of my hospital bed.

I was 34 years old, sore as hell and just wanted to get home to my babies. But I felt so lucky. I was given a gift that my mother was never offered, or even aware of. For that, I am eternally grateful. Grateful I would be around for my two boys (spoiler alert: and my daughter who would join us a couple years later via adoption). Grateful to raise them and to love them and to show them I would do whatever it takes to be the mother they deserve.

That surgery was followed by more reconstruction, a complete hysterectomy, and even, years later, more reconstructive surgery. Was it easy? Hell no. But not once have I looked back and seen it as anything other than the gift it was. It was the catalyst for turning what once was a "poor me" victim mentality into what it is today -- filled with gratitude.

It was during that experience that I saw the opportunity to be who I was meant to be, someone who shares her own story to connect with others who may be going through their own overwhelming challenges, offering them perspective and perhaps a little light of hope. Over the following months and years, I would field calls, emails, and texts from friends who would know someone who might also carry the genetic mutation, would I be open to talking with them?

Absolutely.

I reveled in my new role of supporting other people through challenges I had personally gone through and overcome. And that's a good thing because the years that followed provided me more than my share of unique circumstances, obstacles that sometimes felt like an ever-present kick in the head -- repeatedly. A grueling international adoption process, an autism diagnosis, multiple ICU visits, financial troubles, losing our dream home, watching my father battle -- and ultimately lose -- to Alzheimer's, and a recent child's diagnosis of a chronic, painful autoimmune disease is sometimes enough to make me want to throw in the towel.

But I refuse to succumb.

While it was the loss of my mother that I had always seen as the single most influential moment in my life, often driving my choices during those first 35 years, I realized it was actually my father's example that truly shaped who I am today. My father had experienced more pain in his life, losing his own father and brother to heart disease years before losing his wife and mother of his 11 children to cancer. He was a 38-year-old elevator repairman and single father, who suffered every day with an unfathomable loss, along with debilitating Rheumatoid Arthritis, when he should have been in the prime of his life.

My father had plenty of reasons to give up. But he had even more reason to keep going. His intense love for his family (spoiler alert: including his new wife and two more children), his perseverance and determination to never give up, those are the qualities that shaped who I wanted to become. While I was so focused for so many years on what I had lost, it was my father who was showing up every day, living by example and displaying daily acts of courage that would inspire his family and community.

It was early 2016 when my father began to approach the end of his life. Three weeks before he died, I sat next to him, watching the NFL playoffs, knowing it could be the last time I would see him alive. He didn't know who I was.

He wasn't sure where he was. It hurt my heart to see him begin to give up. But even through the pain, you could see a hint of my father's indomitable spirit rise up and shine through. He kept repeating the same words over and over.

It's been a wonderful life.

His memory was all but gone. His life was nearing the end, yet he still could find the gratitude for what had been. My father chose -- even if not consciously -- gratitude. The best way to honor his legacy is for me to choose gratitude too.

Life can kick us around once in awhile. It's crazy to believe we can live without adversity. But it's that adversity that has actually brought me to my own purpose, passion, and peace. I have faced the dragon and I'm still standing. I no longer look at my personal challenges with that "why me?" attitude, but see them all as an opportunity to become more of the person I'm meant to be -- to choose gratitude above all else.

While I'm still a work in progress, I choose to allow my challenges to shape me in a way that allows me to be of service to others. I choose to look at the mountain that lies ahead step by step, instead of feeling buried by the work required to reach the peak. I choose to be happy in the journey.

Today, I'm the founder of a community of women over 40, sharing my personal experience and expert connections to help other women thrive in their own lives through the choices they make. I'm still married to the love of my life and the proud mother of two teenage boys and a tween daughter. I'm eternally grateful for this messy, sometimes complicated, imperfect life. I'm grateful for all I've been given, within me and around me. And I'm grateful for the opportunity to share this small part of my story with you, the reader. Because through the pain and suffering, growth and personal transformation, one thing remains true...

It's been a wonderful life.

Gratitude and Acknowledgements from the author:

<u>Jackie MacDougall</u>

Jeff MacDougall

Cody MacDougall

Brady MacDougall

Lucy MacDougall

The Lucky 13

Robert Morgan

Janice Morgan

The Forty Thrive Community

About Jackie MacDougall

Born and raised in Boston, Jackie MacDougall packed everything she owned (with $700 bucks to her name) and hit the road for Los Angeles. Since then, she's worked for over two decades in TV and digital marketing, creating content for women with some of the most recognizable and innovative names in entertainment like Queen Latifah, Harry Connick Jr., Tyra Banks, Chrissy Teigen, and Sharon Osbourne.

While her passion for all things entertainment brought her to LA, it's what she's experienced personally and professionally that brought her true purpose. Now instead of just creating content for others to market to women, the blogger and community builder taps into her own personal insight and voice to connect with women — online and in person — helping them find their own distinct voices and use that voice in a way that's authentic and effective.

Jackie, the founder of Forty Thrive and host of the Forty Thrive podcast, lives in the Los Angeles area with her husband and three kids.

Emily Clark

"If my mind can conceive it, and my heart can believe it-then I can achieve it."- Muhammad Ali

Drinks Life

By: Emily Clark

Who am I?

The guilt, the regret, all the questions that you have to answer the next morning. How did I get to this point? Blacking out. Not remembering. Having to check my phone to see the pictures from the previous night to piece it all back together. The dreaded scrolling through text messages to see who I sent a message to and what I had said. Anxiety and embarrassment set in and I can barely function, how am I going to get through this day? Maybe if I just roll over and sleep a little longer I will wake up feeling different. An hour passes, and nothing changes. Well, I guess the only way to make it go away is a little hair of the dog. I drag myself out of bed, throw on the first clothes I can find and a hat to hide the mess of the night before. That first "leveling drink" gets me back to where I need to be. Feeling good, the shakiness is wearing off and the happiness is returning. It looks like we just moved into day drinking, having fun and being the life of the party. Rinse repeat and this became the new norm. How did I get to this point? How do you break the cycle? You are broken, and this is what takes the pain away. This temporary happiness becomes a false reality, and this is all you know.

There is a point that the only way you can be happy is when you are out, the drinks, the music, the people and this is what you look forward to. Escaping dealing with what is going on the inside, burying it deeper and deeper. There is a point where you don't know how you can continue to do this, but you also don't know how to change. How many times can you hit what you think is rock bottom before you decide to make a change. Is this really who I am or how do I redefine myself?

Your life walks out the door

What you think is going to be your forever turns out to be a no longer. After 10 years, giving up your life for another person to achieve their goals and dreams, always putting yours to the side to give and give because that is what you do. You find yourself alone, all over again with no explanation. You are a fighter and a fixer, then poof, the one you gave your whole life to walks out the door. You crumble, you fall apart at the seams, how can this be happening? What did I do to deserve this? I just gave up a life I knew a year ago and now I was completely abandoned. I will never be able to explain those feelings. There is a feeling of being alone, but this was something I had never felt before. Confusion and isolation. You have completely lost yourself in the evolution of this relationship, you are a goal-driven professional but little by little you start to lose that over the years. Who do you become? You become what you think will make the relationship better, copasetic. Do you even know what makes you happy anymore? I start to wonder, how do I move on from this? There is so much self blame, what could I have done differently? Starting over at the age of 42, where would I even begin? Now what? How do I pick myself up when I am broken into a million pieces? I have been knocked down many times but I always manage to rise up. I feel like this is starting to become a pattern. I'm tired of losing myself, rebuilding and starting over.

What to do next? Do I move back to California where I have the most amazing support group between my friends and my amazing FitFam, this has always been my anchor, it is what keeps me sane. Then again, the only downfall of Sacramento is that is where we got married, bought our first home, and created our life together. Will it be too fresh and too hard to let go and heal? Or do I go back to where I started and always seem to return, Scottsdale, where the sun is always shining? It has been 12 years since I left, that will for sure be a new start. This seems to be a no brainer, back to Scottsdale I go. I started putting the wheels in motion to make it back to Arizona. After many months of riding solo and trying to just get by, day by day, it's finally time to pick up and leave the rainy dreary Seattle, it couldn't come soon enough.

Broken Heart/ Rock Bottom

After landing in this new life, I start enjoying the freedom and endless fun! New people, new places, a clean fresh start. Seriously having the time of my life, every day is a party. For me, too much of a good thing tends to lead to toxic relationships. Now looking back on my past relationships this could very well be the cause for rocky points in my life.

Waking up at 3 am with a panic attack, your heart racing............what do you do? You are alone and scared, afraid you are having a heart attack, but what do you do? Why of course, you call your bartender because he is the only one you know is awake. Is this rock bottom? Putting yourself in compromising positions? You know better than this, you were raised differently than this. Your relationships with those that mean the most to you start to fade, you start to separate yourself because you are embarrassed about what you are doing. You don't want anyone to worry, you think you are in control.

When was enough, enough? What does it take before you make changes? When you have hit so many rock bottoms that you really don't know how much lower you can go.

I was physically a mess, tired of not remembering what I did, tired of wasting my life repeating the same things, scared about putting myself in unsafe and vulnerable positions. I knew that I was not that person. Deep down inside I knew that I was destined for something else, something more. When people ask me what I wanted to be, my answer was always "a success story"!

If you don't have your health, you don't have shit" - Dad

After dealing with a racing heart and feeling like I was having a heart attack it turns out that my heart was truly broken. I was diagnosed with Right Ventricular Outflow Tract Tachycardia and went through a procedure to attempt to fix it.

After my heart procedure, it was time to test out the ticker and see if I could start running again without issues. Had it worked? Would I be able to start putting my health first? After a couple of runs, I was fixed, it had worked despite my cells being in a hard to reach spot, it had worked! I was super freaking excited, this was it, it was finally my time again.

As I was scrolling through Facebook one night, I stumbled upon a post about alcohol. As I was reading the comments, I found a book recommendation. I never thought I really had a "problem" with drinking it was just something I did, and it had become part of what I did, and who I was. If I was sad, a drink would make me happy. If was stressed a drink would make me relax. If I was celebrating something, I was celebrating with a shot, it was always cheers for me!

I decided to download the book recommendation and listen during my runs. As I listened to the book it really hit home with me. I never considered myself an alcoholic, but I do know that I had an unhealthy relationship with it. I felt like I didn't want to define myself as having a problem, but I did know that I wanted to do better. Learning what the effects of binge drinking are on your heart I realized that I was given a second chance. I just got my heart unbroken and I needed to take care of it.

I had to take a deep look at what I was doing to myself and what I wanted out of my life. I had the power to write, or in my case re-write my own story. One good decision after the next will lead to good habits and that will turn into your life, your new normal. The first step, I decided that it was time to put drinking to the side, to really let myself feel, stop numbing the pain. I committed to doing Dry July, 30 days without alcohol. I told myself, you can do anything, plus it's only 30 days.

Dry July

I could write a whole book about my experiment with sobriety, but there are a few things that I want to touch on about these 30 days. First, it was hard! As someone who was a daily drinker, it was not an easy task, but once I got over the habit of wanting to have a drink to fix everything it got easier. I also started to discover that I really did, in fact, enjoy being by myself. I am a 99% extrovert and I thrive on being around others to fuel my fire. Now I was learning to really enjoy my own company and create my fire within. As it turns out, sober Emily is pretty awesome!

With the absence of alcohol in my life I started focusing on goals that I wanted to accomplish. I was back at the gym and I putting myself first. Running, boxing and playing softball have always been my jam. If I'm sad, if I'm grumpy, if I'm tired, all this can be now be fixed with a really good sweat session.

During this process I also found out who my true friends were when you eliminate something toxic out of your life, those who only had that in common with you, also disappear. It was a hard fact to swallow but the people who are your true friends will stick with you and share goals and achievements with you.

Having a clear mind I started to get back who I truly was. I make lists, I cross them off, I set goals and I crush them. This is who I am, and this is how I work, end of story. I needed a goal, something to work towards personally, struggling with my weight throughout my life I needed something other than to lose weight as a goal. What was I going to do next? I had run several half marathons and never in my life thought I would be able to run a full marathon, 26.2 miles are you freaking kidding me? Every time I finished a half marathon, I would ask myself, do you think you could do another 13.1 miles right now? Absolutely not! A friend and I were chatting, and she suggested that I run the CIM, California International Marathon, she was doing it, and we were both like-minded and she said, "you CAN do it". I thought to myself.......I can??? So there the goal was born, as simple as someone else believing in me, made me believe in myself.

"You can do anything you set your mind to…." My Mom and Eminem

Finding Myself through Training

After mapping out my training plan it was time to get to work. I think being dedicated to this training is what really allowed me to find myself. Long runs were on Saturdays, so this helped me break my weekend pattern.

It used to be, wow I made it through the week, it's Friday, or what we called *F-Off Friday*. F-Off Friday would lead to hangover Saturday and that in turn would spiral into day drinking Saturday, possibly a nap and there was born rebound Saturday night. Insert some guilt and regret Sunday which could lead to leveling out brunch and Sunday Funday. Monday was always a struggle and there were mornings I really didn't know how I was going to get through the day.

Knowing that I had to be in prime condition for my long run on Saturday my Friday night turned into rest, fueling my body right, and early to bed so I could rise early. Having this accountability, knowing the importance of the long run set the tone for my entire weekend. I would allow myself some flexibility on Saturday night, but I found that during Dry July, the invitations to go out were less frequent and I was quite content with just being by myself. I never thought I would be at that point, from a girl who used to eat and drink at the hotel bar across the street every single day. My health was finally a priority. I had to get to the point where it was something that I wanted. I was finally there! This was for ME, this is was what made it stick.

This process and the training removed all toxic elements from my life and brought me closer to people who had similar goals and we developed a deeper friendship based on training, fitness, crushing life and not based on going out and drinking to not remember. The party lifestyle was out and becoming an athlete became my focus.

26.2

After completing my first marathon I realized that I was not the same person. I had in fact transformed, and it was this goal, the training, and the dedication that I made myself a priority and let nothing get in the way. Through the months of training, I had obstacles, but I made plans and stuck to it. The support group that I had during the process was instrumental. If you aren't happy with where you are, YOU have the ability to change it.

You can change, but you have to want it for you. It's not easy but it's worth it. Everyone deals with adversity and tragedy differently but it's how you come back from it that matters. How do you rise up?

The one thing that I want everyone to know is that truly anything is possible, but also, it's time to break this pattern that society put upon us, the social pressure that you have to drink to have fun. Absolutely not the truth, you can in fact, I'm living proof, have fun without drinking......it's all a perception. Alcohol actually gave me a false perception of what happiness was, it was a vicious cycle. Removing it from the equation made me realize that I could laugh without a shot, I could wake up refreshed, I could conquer my fear of missing out and accomplish my goals, one step at a time!

What's Next?

I am hoping that this brief look into one of many of my journeys will help one person out there realize that they are worth it to make the change. You can, in fact, do anything you put your mind to, that it all boils down to sucking it up, putting on your big girl panties, making a plan, and crushing the hell out of that goal. It's not for the weak but you are way stronger than you think you are. Don't fake the funk, you can't have one foot in your old life and one foot in the life you want. You have to make the decision, of course, you may have to keep trying over and over again, but freaking do it! What are you waiting for, your life is going to keep moving on, and you will regret not taking the step sooner. I still believe that everything in your life happens for a reason and I was able to achieve these goals because I was meant to help and inspire someone to be better and do better.

This chapter was just the start. There are many more stories, triumphs, and lessons learned, some that make me shake my head but I know they need to be shared. The good, the bad, and the WTF? Stay tuned for a bigger glimpse into my transformation and how I redefined myself after being knocked down.

PRESENTED BY: DAWN BORNHEIMER

Gratitude and Acknowledgements from the author:

<u>Emily Clark</u>

Mom and Dad

Mindy Foulger

Jessa Woodward

Sarah Keating

Remy Clark

Dennis Guerra

Alex Craviotto

Lauren Bland

Kadin Brueske

About Emily Clark

Emily Clark is a professional in the Architecture, Engineering and Construction industry. Her professional life has centered around positively impacting the communities in which she has lived through Design and Architecture. Her current role as the Director of Services has enabled her to take her experiences in the industry and push her team of technical specialists to provide stellar services and to help improve processes for major design firms across the United States. Through public speaking and engaging with other industry leaders, she is able to share her passion for technology and people.

In her personal life, Emily is a badass who has realized that her self-worth is more important than the instant gratification received from society's push toward certain lifestyle choices. She puts her mind to the goals she creates and sets about crushing them one by one. Emily is driven by constant improvement and being the best freaking version of herself yet. She will inspire you, make you laugh and make you realize that you are not alone in this crazy world.

www.shedrinkslife.com

PRESENTED BY: DAWN BORNHEIMER

Kim LaMontagne

"Hope Anchors the Soul"

Sometimes To Live Is An Act of Courage

By: Kim LaMontagne

July 16, 2009, was a pivotal day in my life. It was a beautiful summer day in New England. I worked in Western New Hampshire that day. My ride home from work was peaceful and stunning. I love driving through that part of the state. Although the ride surrounded me with beauty, my internal mental well being was severely out of alignment. In the years leading up to this day, I had carried an unbearable silent burden. A burden, so heavy that at times, I felt like I would break. A burden many layers of deep shame, fear, worthlessness, and guilt. A burden that made me feel like an outcast and someone who didn't deserve space on this earth.

By 4:45 pm on that day, I was crying uncontrollably in the parking lot of the Mall of New Hampshire in Manchester. I decided it was the day I was going to face my fears and expose a part of me that I had hidden for years. I called my doctor's office to make an appointment for a personal matter. Although, I did not expect to get a same day appointment, the stars aligned for me that day. There was an appointment available at 5:15 pm with the new male nurse practitioner. What I was going to share was so vulnerable and raw. I was unsure if I wanted to see a male practitioner I had never seen before. I decided to take a leap of faith.

When he entered the room and asked why I had come to see him, I broke down in tears. I was paralyzed and not able to speak for several minutes. Once I was able to gain my composure, I shared that I had been struggling for years with alcohol abuse, major depression, anxiety, and suicidal thoughts. I was a wine drinker. I drank to numb the feeling of shame and worthlessness. Although I was a self-imposed outcast, I was always the one to say "let's have a party". I was also the one who constantly blacked out and woke up the next day feeling physically awful and guilty because I had too much to drink. I now recognize this guilt as shame and loss of identity because I had to drink every day.

After sharing my deepest darkest secret with the nurse practitioner, he clenched his hands together, looked me *directly in the eye* and said, "I am going to help you". He left the room and returned with brochures and sample medications. We discussed how to effectively treat the co-occurring illnesses of depression and alcohol abuse disorder. He prescribed medications and closely monitored my progress. I committed to weekly counseling and began going to AA meetings. He spent forty-five minutes with me that day. Within those four walls of the exam room, it was as if no one in the world existed at that time except me. He gave me hope and more importantly, he did not have any judgment. He viewed my ailment as a treatable disease and gave me the tools and support I needed to transition into the new me. It was a judgment-free zone.

Recovery was very difficult. I experienced many side effects from the medication including nausea and loss of appetite. I had difficulty grocery shopping because the sight and smell of food made me nauseous. After removing the alcohol from my diet, my craving for sugar became intense. For one year, my diet consisted of ice coffee, ice cream and all sugar. I lost 25 pounds and looked frail, fragile and gaunt. I had difficulty sleeping and was exhausted every day. Family and friends expressed concern about me. To avoid admitting to my pain, my typical response was, "I'm fine". During this time, my 14-year marriage was crumbling and finally ended in 2010.

During the intense battle, I remained a top performing, award-winning, Senior Consultant in my full-time job. I work remotely which made it easy to hide my secret from coworkers. I saw my coworkers once or twice a year.

From their vantage point, I was an outstanding top performing employee who had it all together. Little did they know, I was suffering alone in a very dark world riddled with guilt, shame, fear, and complete emptiness. I was afraid to share my illness because of shame, stigma, and fear of losing my job. I was fighting an exhausting physical and mental battle on the inside but wearing a mask every day on the outside to hide it. I suffered in complete silence.

I began a long term relationship and the next several years were good. My mental health was under control, my cravings for alcohol virtually disappeared, I was active in AA and seeing a therapist regularly. Work was busy, my daughter was in college, I was in love and life was good. In 2012, I learned the nurse practitioner was leaving the practice to transition into a new role. I was devastated. I started seeing a new provider, but the connection just wasn't there and I began avoiding my appointments. Later that year, I made the decision to stop my medication because "I was feeling good". I did this by weaning off my prescription medication and transitioning over to all-natural supplements. Weaning off the medication was difficult. I experienced nausea and restlessness, but eventually, I settled into a new balance.

In 2013, my living arrangement changed. I found myself living alone. My daughter was in college and my boyfriend had relocated to California to care for his ailing mother. He was my rock and he was gone. At first, it was challenging, but over time I got used to the solitude. I began to crave the alone time and would avoid interacting with people. My job involved face to face interaction and engagement and I continued to be a high performer. To accomplish this, I put on a mask of happiness to hide the intense pain I was feeling. At the end of the day, I would remove the mask and retreat into my world of solitude and darkness. This was the only way I could get the job done. I avoided activities and invitations and developed a fear of going out at night.

During this time, I began having intense thoughts of suicide. Each day I would wake up and suicide was the first thought on my mind. Because I lived alone and didn't want to burden anyone, I suffered in silence and never asked for help. Texting is wonderful because it allowed me to hide behind technology and fool everyone into believing I was great. Many days I would stay inside and cry. Other days, I would go for a walk and try to decide which car to jump in front of. I had constant thoughts of driving off the road or into a river. Anything was better than being stuck in a mind that was being bombarded by thoughts of worthlessness, shame, guilt, embarrassment, and suicide. Yet, I continued. Day by day and sometimes minute by minute. Darkness became my new normal. I believed that was the way life was supposed to be. That was my brain playing tricks on me.

Trigger Warning:

On one dark day in 2013, I reached my lowest point. I was alone in my home getting ready to paint a dining room that was being converted into a bedroom. In the corner, there was a closet that was being framed out with exposed 2x4's. To me, those 2x4's screamed as the perfect place to hang something and that something was me. Since I lived alone, I was worried how long it would take to be found if I did the unthinkable. I drafted a text message to my neighbor asking him to call the local police but not to come into my house. During that time, I systematically went through my list of loved ones, friends and colleagues and could justify how everyone would be better off without me. At that time, I could rationalize why my boyfriend, father, brother, and sister would be fine without me. My co-workers would be shocked, but they would be fine and so would all my friends. When I got to my daughter, that is when I realized that my life is worth living and I need to stay here for her and subsequently for me. I sat on the floor and cried. I screamed, "where did my hopes and dreams go, what happened to the light in my eyes, how did I end up at the bottom of this deep dark hole of depression"? I remained silent about my struggles. Several times over the course of 2013, I considered checking into the Emotional Care unit at my local hospital, but I was too ashamed to ask for help. Instead, I remained silent because of fear, shame, and stigma.

In 2014, my daughter graduated from college and moved home. While they were away, I developed obsessive-compulsive disorder and was very specific about the cleanliness and arrangement of my house. I was concerned about cohabiting again because I feared they would see my illness. When I lived alone, I could hide my illness and take the mask off at the end of the day and crumble. When they moved home, I had to stay strong and happy all the time. It was exhausting for me. They began to see the physical and mental signs of my depression and became worried. My boyfriend was my biggest supporter but I never let him know the level of pain I was experiencing. At that time, I began communicating with my sister more and started sharing my struggles with her. She was also going through a very difficult time in her life. One day I asked her if she ever felt like ending it all. She was up against so many struggles. It made sense to me that she would feel suicidal too. When I asked her the question, "don't you feel like just ending it all", she looked me straight into my eyes and said, "NO", I have never thought of that! That was the moment I knew, I needed to seek help and that my depression was out of control.

Later that evening, while preparing to sit down to dinner, my father called. I asked if I could call him back after dinner. In a very stern voice, he said NO, we are going to talk right now. He informed me that my sister reached out to alert him of the severity of my depression and suicidal thoughts. He was very concerned. My sister and father do not have a close relationship. For my sister to have reached out to my father with this concern was another indicator that I needed help. My father told me if I ever had suicidal feelings or needed help, he would be there for me in a minute. This is the same father I had recently justified would be ok without me.

In 2015, I found a new nurse practitioner at my doctor's office who specialized in mental health. She created that nonjudgmental loving environment for me again. I am so thankful for her. I began a regular course of antidepressants and anti-anxiety medications and began to turn the corner but still wasn't out of the woods yet.

During this time, I felt a strong pull to engage in a weekend retreat to focus on self-care and finding my true self. It wasn't until 2016 that I finally signed up for my first retreat.

In the spring of 2016, my director at work had noticed that things were "off" with me. Because of this, she made a special day trip to Boston from New Jersey to talk with me. I decided to finally be honest about the struggle I had been battling on my own. She was shocked and saddened that I had struggled so long without asking for help. She was encouraging and nonjudgmental and provided me with great support. Additionally, she recognized the level of work accomplishments I had achieved while fighting this invisible battle. She rewarded me by giving me the Friday before and the Tuesday after Memorial Day Weekend off from work and instructed me to take time for myself. This gave me a 5-day weekend and the stars aligned for me again.

I googled, "Memorial Day weekend 2016, spiritual retreats" and found The Work of Byron Katie. I did not know anything about Byron Katie, but when I read her bio, it spoke to me and I knew I had to see her. She lived with depression and suicidal thoughts until she had an awakening and discovered "The Work". I signed up for the retreat and drove from NH to Rhinebeck NY for the 4-day retreat.

Byron Katie's work saved my life and freed me from a life of suicidal, harmful and negative thoughts. Her process called, "The Work" taught me how to question my thoughts. It allowed me to understand that many of the thoughts I had been experiencing, were created by me and 100% not true. Over the course of the weekend, I witnessed individuals approaching the stage with a thought or a belief that was so unbearable that it was overtaking their life. After working with Katie, individuals were left with a new found sense of hope and freedom. Stories of trauma, despair, loss, fear, anxiety and other emotional anchors were shared that weekend. I felt something change that weekend. Something had shifted. I felt the light inside of me turn back on again. I had a spark of hope for the first time in many years. It was the turning point in my healing.

From that weekend forward, I become healthier by the minute. I could feel the shift occurring both physically and mentally. In August 2016, I went to another retreat and met another angel who changed my life… singer, songwriter and author, Karen Drucker. Karen's music flowed through me like warming fluids of an IV. One song at time, her music filled the cracks and crevices of my soul. Songs such as "I Am a Gift", "I Don't Have to Be Perfect" and "I Am Open", gave me a newfound love for myself. Her music brought me back to life.

In November 2016, I learned about the non-profit organization, National Alliance on Mental Illness (NAMI). I signed up for a weekend training for the NAMI, In Our Own Voice Program where I learned to share my story of recovery. I felt empowered and passionate about sharing my story. I also engaged in NAMI Advocacy training and became certified as a support group facilitator and Family-to-Family teacher.

As part of my graduate MBA capstone, I collaborated with NAMI, MA to analyze the outcome of their grant-funded CEOs Against Stigma Campaign. CEOs Against Stigma is a statewide campaign designed to reduce the negative impact of stigma in the workplace by bringing the reality of mental illness out of the shadows.

In 2018, I became a Speaker, Advisory Board Member and Ambassador for Worth Living Mental Health. Recently, I was named as a member of the Dartmouth Hitchcock Health System, Campaign to Combat Stigma and Discrimination in Behavioral Health. I volunteer frequently at my local hospital by sharing my story with patients in the inpatient and partial hospitalization program (PHP).

My story of being a high functioning, top performing businesswoman, balancing a career and family, while fighting (and hiding) mental illness has resonated with many. I fought my battle alone because I was afraid of the stigma. Especially in the workplace. My story is not unique. What is unique is that I am brave enough to share and be vulnerable. No one should suffer in silence. We need to start the conversation now about mental health.

Gratitude and Acknowledgements from the author:

<u>Kim LaMontagne</u>
Pierre Melzer

Ashyln Rowe

Wendy Renna

Bill Bolton

Chuck Bolton

Lynn Bolton

Stacey Rao

Steve Gutwillig, NP

Karen Drucker

Byron Katie

My Entire Women Tribe

About Kim LaMontagne

Kim LaMontagne has devoted her life to helping others survive and thrive in the face of mental illness. After suffering in silence with anxiety, major depression, suicidal thoughts, and alcohol abuse disorder, Kim has found recovery and a life of true happiness.

A consistent 'top performer' and winner of several Director's and Peer Choice Awards within her organization, Kim suffered alone the workplace because of shame and fear of stigma. Her professional performance never wavered, but inside she was broken, empty and on the verge of giving up. Kim shares her story of recovery to help others find the courage, power, and strength to rise above the fear, stigma and shame of mental illness.

Kim is a Speaker, Teacher and Advocate with National Alliance on Mental Illness, New Hampshire chapter, an Ambassador, Speaker and Member of the Advisory Board of Worth Living Mental Health, a Member of the Dartmouth Hitchcock Health System Campaign to Combat Stigma and Discrimination in Behavioral Health, Contributing Author and Survivor.

She is a frequent speaker at conferences and conducts onsite workplace mental health presentations. She has written several blogs about mental health and recently conducted her first podcast.

Kim believes we must start the conversation now about mental health.

Especially in the workplace.   Life is Worth Living.

Kim@kimlamontagne.net

www.kimlamontagne.net

Follow Kim on Facebook, LinkedIn, and Instagram

PRESENTED BY: DAWN BORNHEIMER

Leia Lewis

"You, yourself, as much as anybody in the entire universe deserve your love and affection." -Buddha

What You Seek, You Shall Find Within

By: Leia Lewis

I remember waking up in this cramped college dorm bed and having no idea how I got there. I felt like I got hit by a bulldozer. My head was throbbing with intense pain, I felt sick to my stomach, and I smelled the aroma of old beer running through the air. I looked next to me to find the guy I had been hanging out with the night before.

All of a sudden this massive feeling of anxiety, guilt, and sensation that I was going to be sick to my stomach came over my whole body. I quietly got up, found my clothes on the floor, my purse and tiptoed out of the room. I couldn't find my shoes anywhere. I could barely think, my whole body was shaking, I drank way too much alcohol the night before, and my head hurt so bad that I had trouble seeing straight. I called my friend who lived on campus nearby who I knew would help.

The next 20 minutes felt like the longest 20 minutes ever. Every worst case thought ran through my head about what had happened last night. I blacked out. I really had no idea what happened. I remember hanging out with the guy,

I remember going to his room, and then nothing else. The fear, the panic, the feelings of shame were so intense.

Finally, my friend arrived and as I got into his car and looked into his eyes, I broke down and began hysterically crying.

Over the next week, I tortured myself. Every bad thought made me feel worse and worse. I wallowed in my misery.

As weeks went by, I stuffed the memory away, 'forgot' it ever happened, and eventually it started to disappear. I didn't tell anyone. I resumed fun college life, drank plenty, went to more frat parties, and acted like that night never happened.

I grew up in central New Jersey with a relatively normal life. I am the oldest of three. My brother is two years younger than me and my sister is about nine and a half years younger. Both my parents are great people. They raised us to think for ourselves, to be independent, to be hardworking and gave us the freedom to make many of our own decisions early in life.

When I was five years old, on Christmas Eve, my family and I headed to a Christmas party that my dad's work hosted each year. My dad worked at a large corporate company at the time and we loved this annual party. Santa would give us a gift before Christmas and I looked forward to this party all year. On the way home from the party that night, our life would change forever.

I must have fallen asleep in my booster seat because all of a sudden I remember waking up to blood-curdling screams. "Bobby, Leia, Timon, are you ok?" "Bobby, are you ok?" "Leia are you ok?" It was like a broken record. My mom kept saying it over and over and over and over. She sounded terrified. I looked for my dad who was sitting in the middle row of our wagon ahead of me. I was in the third row in the back. My dad had a broken leg at the time with a long cast up over his knee so he was seated sideways on the seat. I saw a line of red blood running down the back of his head. He wasn't answering my mom. The image of that blood running down his head is forever ingrained in my memory.

What happened next, I'm not really sure. I remember waking up in a hospital bed all alone. There were a ton of doctors and nurses all around me asking me questions. All I remember is worrying where my mom, my dad, and my brother was. I didn't feel any pain. I didn't think I was hurt. I was told we were in a car accident.

The next few weeks were a blur. A good family friend of my parents picked me up from the hospital that same day and brought me to their house. Christmas morning I woke up alone without my family having no idea if they were ok.

Looking back at this time as an adult, I must have been in a state of fear. After the accident, I have very few memories of my life over the next few years. My childhood from age 5-7 is so blurry. I don't remember my parents coming home from the hospital, or where I went to school, who my friends were, or even what I liked to do. As an adult, after some therapy, I discovered that the accident was a pivotal event of trauma in my life. I realized that the accident was so traumatic for me as a child, that my brain as a protective mechanism, erased the memories.

By the time I got to 5th or 6th grade, I had developed an intense desire to do well in school. I became a perfectionist. I strived to do the best I could, get good grades, get into honors classes in middle school, get into AP high school classes and worked hard to get a great SAT score. I desired to be popular and I was. I was an athlete and had many friends.

Because I was obsessed with doing well, I did well. I graduated at the top of my high school class, school class and graduated college from Rutgers College with a top GPA.

Fast forward some years, after graduating from college, and getting a great job at a top corporate insurance company, getting engaged to my amazing boyfriend, life was good! I had the man of my dreams, I had a great job, we were happy, and I was making good money, what more could you ask for!

We bought our first house together about a year later and got married a year after that. I was loving my job, advancing in my career, happily married, and we were making really good money.

I started to become obsessed with my career. I pushed harder, worked more, went for promotions, got some, and was feeling rewarded. The harder I worked, the better I felt. The more I achieved, the happier I got.

Our first baby girl, Molly arrived a few years later! The moment I looked at her eyes, the moment I saw her, my life changed. I had this undying love for this little being that I created and I had no idea how I could possibly love someone so much. It was a different kind of love. A love that felt more powerful than I had ever had before.

A few years later, we got pregnant again. I remember walking into the doctor to have my first appointment and being told we were going to have our ultrasound the same day. As the ultrasound tech examined me, all of a sudden, she turned the screen and said 'well, you have two babies! You are having twins!' I laughed so hard I couldn't breathe. Meanwhile, my husband was hyperventilating!

Life surely changed when we found out we were having two babies not one. Everything in our life was too small, needed upgrades, or changes. I was so excited but terrified at the same time.

The day I looked at and held my twins, Izzy and Ellie, was another one of those most amazing memories you never forgot. How on earth did I create these two amazing beings? How is it possible to have two perfect babies? How am I so lucky?

Mom life became quickly hard. Having a toddler and a newborn is hard. Having a toddler and 2 newborns is even harder. Of course, I did the best I could, I was a rockstar mama, I breastfed both babies at the same time, took charge of getting them on a schedule and they were thankfully really good babies.

A few months later, despite all that I was doing to keep up, I noticed how sad I was. I was really anxious all the time, short-fused, negative, night times for us were hell from 6-9pm. I went back to work full time when the twins were 5 months old and right around that time too my husband switched to working nights. I felt so exhausted and stressed and alone.

I started to dread my life. I started to feel resentment. I started to feel unhappy. I took a voluntary demotion at work because I just couldn't keep up. I didn't want to let my family down and didn't want to let my career down either. I started to drink wine more regularly each night. I ate poorly. I would spend my evenings after bedtime, drinking wine, eating nachos or take out pizza, immersing myself in Vampire Diaries, Grey's Anatomy, and Scandal. I would drink wine and pretend like my life was like my favorite tv shows.

My anxiety continued to get worse. I was in denial for sure. I thought everyone who had kids felt the same way. But ultimately, I went to a doctor and they diagnosed me with Postpartum Depression. Hearing that label was a shock to my ego. I was mortified and embarrassed. I was ashamed to tell anyone and even admit to myself I was depressed because it made me feel weak. So I didn't tell anyone.

Within a few more years of repeating this pattern of self-destructive behavior, I had gained about 25-30 extra pounds. My energy levels were rock bottom. I woke up each day with a hangover. I woke up thinking this can't be it? This can't be the way life is meant to be lived. I hated my body, I hated my life, myself, my kids felt like a chore, my marriage had deteriorated, we were having massive financial issues, spending way too much money on things that would make us 'happy'.

One day after feeling like enough was enough, I made the decision to start taking care of myself.

I began a workout program at home in my basement. I did it at night late after the girls were in bed, after a long day at work, and gave it my all. The sweat that came off my body those first few weeks was like I was back at high school soccer boot camp. I felt like I was going to die. My body was so sore I could barely move. But I had this drive, this determination, this need to do this for me. For the first time in my life, in a really long time, I felt pushed and pulled all at the same time. I was not going to quit on me. I had quit on me for way too long in life.

Day by day, I got stronger. The weight came off. My

energy skyrocketed. My confidence started to bloom. I started to learn about how to eat properly. What foods were good for my body, that really fueled it. I started to change my habits and replaced the poor ones I had been making with good ones. This shake that my friend told me I needed to drink that would restore and refuel my body, was making me feel alive again.

Each day that passed by, I gained confidence that I could keep going. I did it yesterday, so I can do it tomorrow. And then I started to tackle some of the small problems in my life. I started to tackle them instead of avoiding them. I started to think that life was more than just the mundane routine. I started to believe in me.

Over the past three years, as I poured into my own cup, as I worked on my body and mind, I realized that my whole life I had been pushing and striving and seeking that THING that would make me feel complete.

Whether it was the attention of a male, or being a perfectionist and getting good grades, working to get into the best college, pushing for a job promotion, buying things, drinking wine nightly and binge-watching tv, eating food to cope with my emotions... they were ALL the same!

These actions were a direct cry for that thing I was TRYING to find. I remember one day, it was early in the morning, I had begun a routine of spending at least 20 minutes each day reading. I don't remember exactly the words that I read, but I remember that breakthrough… the overwhelming clarity that all that had happened in my life, all that I have been through, all the obstacles and victories were there to teach me a lesson. I remember this feeling of 'holy cow' I am doing it ALL wrong.

Life is not about WHAT you acquire, the house you have, the money you earn, the things you get, the titles you have. While there is nothing wrong with wanting those things and getting them … THEY do not define you.

I had been searching for something for so many years that I already had.

As I began to discover this inner strength and love for myself, I became obsessed with sharing this message! I have dedicated the last 3 years of my life to sharing this. I have put my energy and time and focus on being the best I can be and teaching others how to do the same.

Last fall, as I was sitting in an arena filled with 12,000 other people at a personal growth event, it hit me like a ton of bricks clearer than ever. My whole life I have been seeking LOVE and HAPPINESS. We all want happiness. We all want to be loved. It is our innate desire as human beings to crave this.

Except, instead of actually chasing love and happiness, I chased success. I chased success because that was easier. I chased success because it was what my family valued. I chased success because that is how I received love and connection as a child. I chased success because I thought it would BRING me love and happiness. I chased attention, connection, drank too much, pushed myself in my career and my current business, all because I just wanted LOVE.

The TRUTH is, I already have all the love inside of me. I am the essence of love. Love is a feeling, it is a belief, and it is within you. Love is meant to be shared, it is meant to urge you to grow, it is meant to push you, scare you, challenge you. If you are not FULLY loving yourself, you are not fully living.

I sat in that arena a few months ago, and felt my heart, felt this beautiful feeling of clarity, felt this power within me, felt this love inside for ME, despite all the flaws, despite my past, despite what I can do better, despite everything, I felt PURE joy for the first time in my life.

You already have everything you always desired within you. Peel away the layers and see it's there for you too! I truly hope that my story has sparked something in you that will encourage you to begin your journey or continue on it to find the love you desire in life which is simply within you already!

Gratitude and Acknowledgements from the author:

<u>Leia Lewis</u>

My husband, Ronnie Lewis

My parents, Bob and Donna Peskin

Erica Nitti Becker

My Business Partners on Team Arise and Team Reveal

Taren Sbardella

Dana Fotiades

About Leia Lewis

Leia Lewis is a mentor, leader, motivated wife, and mother of three beautiful girls. After spending 12 years in Corporate America, Leia decided climbing the corporate ladder was not worth sacrificing her own well being and that of her family. She took control of her life, invested in herself both personally and professionally, discovering tools that allowed her to feel alive again. For the past 3+ years, Leia has devoted herself to helping women lose weight, unblock mental barriers, and create empowering habits. She has created a powerful online community to support women along their journey. Leia is passionate about teaching others that their mind is capable of magnificent things and comfort zones are meant to be crushed.

Leia has plans to write her own book in the future and continues to spread her mission of women empowerment and vulnerability on social media. You can connect with her on Instagram @leialewisfitness and at leialewisfitness.com.

Natasha Novak

"Life doesn't have to be perfect to be wonderful" - Annette Funicello

Let Life Be

By: Natasha Novak

Life is balancing act. For me like most everyone at some point I'm sure. One week I will feel like that guy in the circus spinning 100 plates all at the same time. Then the next week it's like a calm quiet mill pond, peaceful and still.

So how do I, you, we find balance in those packed full days and generally everyday life to get to the end of that day and smile and say, today was a great day, ok a little optimistic, today I made it through the day!

I am a Mom to two wonderful children, Wife and business owner. My goal in writing this is to share my own experiences with you, in what has helped me find the balance of all my titles and also just being me, and being able to embrace life as it changes through the different phases in our lives, it takes work, and dedication but you deserve to live your best life.

I am a big believer in everything happens for a reason and honestly whether good, bad or indifferent each or those things helps us grow a little, become stronger and ultimately teaches us a new lesson, the key is to embrace these situations as they are, take one step at a time but keep on moving forward.

A Bit About Me

I grew up in the UK, and was very lucky and blessed with a wonderful family and friends. I always made friends easily, and never felt that was a struggle.

My Mum moved the USA when I was 19 years old, and of course being 19 years old and thinking i probably knew it all, did not want to go as had all my friends right there, I was also working on my four year apprenticeship as well and wanted to complete that and gain some qualifications and experience in my chosen field of Health and Fitness.

I would visit my Mum in small town Wisconsin regularly, one or two times a year for a couple weeks and fell in love with it too, and after completing my apprenticeship along with multiple qualifications, and at 21 felt like I too wanted to make the move across the pond. I applied for my visa in the year 2001, the process seemed to drag on forever, and many life events, and changes later, including changing careers to work in the Insurance field, which was initially a stop gap to free up my time to enable me to go back to school in the evenings, to complete my teaching certificate, which I did complete, and went on to teach at the local College for 2 years, but my role changed at the Insurance company and was offered a promotion, so I took it, and am still in the Insurance field to this day.

I also met someone, a couple years later had a baby, and then broke up. And before I knew it it was the end of the year 2009 and the United States Embassy had sent me a letter for mine and my son's appointment to get our Green Cards, to enable us to move across the world together. We went to that appointment in January 2010 and moved in the April. I handed in my notice at my job I had been at for 8 years, I packed up all our belongings, and off we went to our whole new life awaiting us.

Life Across the Pond: Lesson One

My son who was 1 years old and I got settled in pretty quick, and within a few weeks, we had all our documentation complete and I was able to apply for jobs. After eight weeks of moving here and being pretty independent and ambitious, I got myself a good paying job. There was a major difference though from my job back home, it was longer hours, and very little vacation, I worked hard though, and after 8 months was promoted to a District Manager, I was able to buy myself a brand new car and felt like I was making here. But however, I missed my son and felt like I was away from him way to much. I made a decision to apply for a job back that would take me back into the insurance world and took a pay cut, but felt I had better flexibility and opportunities ahead of me, and after two years I secured my own Insurance Agency and am became a business owner, which is still my current occupation.

I had many mental battles at this job too, it's not only hard making it in business world, hiring, training, tough conversations, long hours, and for me mainy the feeling of having took a step back in my career, was a struggle for a very long time. But as life has progressed and throwing in there, a husband and another baby, I take a step back reflect, and am beyond grateful for how life has turned out so far. This job not only enables me to decide when I work and whom I work with. It allowed me to bring my new baby to work with me, which I did until she was one year old, and I also come and go as I need to. This is key for me as a parent. I come in half an hour later than the opening time, as take my children to daycare and school, and then take myself to the gym, I don't have to miss out on school trips, or events, and take a day off each week in summer to spend with my kids and do something fun.

The flexibility I have created is better than any paycheck, or promotion I have ever received. But as I said it took a long time for me to mentally get to this point, and still have that mental battle in my head, I should be at work when I am at home with my family, and the feeling I should be with the family when I am at work, or doing house work etc. But I think that battle I know not only I have, but many other woman I have spoke to or read in their books.

Friends and Tribe: Lesson Two

Another area of my life I have felt a huge gap in since moving here to the United States was in my personal relationships; specifically having a deep friendship or connection with a girlfriend.

Back home I had those friendships, you know the ones I'm talking about, you could go months without talking to each other but the minute you see each other it is like you had seen each other just yesterday, and just pick right back up where you left off and to this day. Its amazing but I can honestly say, I still get that feeling when I go home each year to visit. I could tell those girls anything, there was never any judgment, bitchyness, just pure love, and yes sometimes harsh but honest truth.

It's hard moving and building new deep friendships, but when I look back the best friends I have back home, they all came into my life without even looking, they just showed up all of a sudden and there they stayed forever.

The internet has been said to be many negative things, but for me it has helped me not only keep in touch with family and friends from back home, but also provided a vehicle for me to create a wonderful tribe of positive, uplifting woman who I know I can go to with anything, bounce ideas off of and get the real honest feedback in return. I am part of a number of groups but only really stay in the ones that bring joy and positivity to my world, I get to chose and that's the wonderful part of social media, you can choose what you let in.

I also have built some amazing friendships from work and working out, and now have a really strong girl connection with the group I workout with in the mornings too. I think it took me to stop hoping and wanting what I had before, and to basically stop living in the past and to really allow myself to live in the moment of my new life. I having lived in the US for nine years now, so it's not really new anymore, but it certainly feels new some days. On those days, I choose to embrace it and love it, without expectation. Once I did this it really opened my eyes and I was able to finally see the true friendships I have built, and although it is not like what I had before, they were never meant to be, they were supposed to be just as they are, and to me it is perfect.

Take Action

My way of thinking and being today did not just happen magically, although sometimes life just happens, it has taken time, effort and work to get to this point, and here are some of the things that have really helped me find my peace and happiness in every aspect of my life.

Make Time for Me

When life is hectic, busy, stressful or whatever it throws at me, making time for myself each day has helped so much. My main thing that I like to do is workout, whether it be functional fitness, running, spinning, yoga or any other thing that gets me moving, this is my thing. I go to the gym Monday through Friday, and there are some days, when there is no school, or a work event that comes up and I can't make it, but for the most part its every week day. There have been some patches in life where I have sacrificed my workout time for "life" and it was rough, I was cranky, resentful, and I couldn't handle stress nowhere near as well.

There are times where it is so difficult to fit it into my day, and then that little feeling of guilt creeps in and I start to think I should be at work or I should be doing this or that, but afterwards I feel like I can tackle anything, and I feel good. Taking time for yourself is never selfish it is essential.

Learn Something New

I love to read, but will be really honest, I was struggling to find the ambition too, at the end of the day by the time I got to bed I was tired and would get half way down a page and fall asleep, and then I felt sad that I was not getting to learn and grow, so I just found a different way and time to get my learning in, I now listen to audible books, and podcasts, I listen whenever I have a longer drive by myself, which actually doesn't happen to often with two children, but when I do I learn. I also listen when I run outside too, it's amazing how distracting a good book is while you run!

I also like to learn from others in person, and online. I have signed up for online leadership courses, and gone to day retreats and even travelled out of state for an all woman retreat, which was amazing and I highly recommend for everyone. I feel like when we are learning, we are growing, and I get the feel fulfilled as a human being.

Take a Step Back

This one is probably my most difficult one, but so very important. Letting myself stop, be still, quiet and meditate. This brings me back, reminds me to stop and smell the roses and be grateful for all the abundance I have around and in my life, and also reminds me to be present in the moment, to play with my children, talk to my Husband and put the electronics away, we live in a fast paced world, dominated by computers, so this is really critical for connection, but can be a challenge, especially for the modern day entrepreneur in me.

I think way to often we live in this hamster wheel, and are continuously running to keep going, without taking a breath, but through the courses I have taken, and through having an app reminder each night on my phone, they have helped me learn this wonderful tool, that I feel has helped open my eyes and to embrace life in a positive light.

I hope these small tips help you in your life, if you too have had these feelings, and that you can use some of the tools I have found have helped me get to the place I am at today.

Don't feel guilty, it's not selfish, but taking the time for you, and sometimes just letting life be you will be amazed at how wonderful it can be!

Gratitude and Acknowledgements from the author:

<u>Natasha Novak</u>

Mum

Gary

Darin

Gemma, Emma, and Sarah

About Natasha Novak

Natasha is a British girl now American citizen too. Business Owner, Mom, wife, with a passion for leadership, developing others and self-development. Having worked in the Insurance industry for more than 16 years, from working for the largest Insurance company in the U.K within corporate leadership and project change roles to now an Independent Business Owner, achieving multiple awards for sales and customer service.

Also having been within the health industry for more than 20 years, she has built a large depth of knowledge and experience, both in not only physical fitness and nutrition but in the mind and spirit too.

A confident leader, speaker, and mentor Natasha has a real passion for helping others and particularly coaching others to be the best they can be within their own roles.

Anna Owusu

"Change is the law of life and those who look only to the past or present are certain to miss the future." John F. Kennedy

Finding Home

By: Anna Owusu

Born into Transition

The year 1980 began a decade of transition all over the world. The world went through a period of drastic metamorphosis with an accompanying rollercoaster of mixed emotions.

In the United States political scene, the Reagan era began with Ronald Reagan being elected as president, in the media world, CNN the very first 24-hour cable news network was about to be launched. Marjorie Matthew's election as first female bishop of any mainline Christian denomination in history was historic and unprecedented! Sadly, that same year gave witness to was music icon, John Lennon's assassination.

Meanwhile, on the global front tensions were building at a fast pace as Iraq declared war on Iran. For the people of Cuba, it was good news! Hope had sprung! The Castro administration gave permission and access to Cubans wanting to immigrate to the United States to do so. Thousands of Cubans made their way to Florida as soon as the next day in hopes of starting a new and better life.

Africa, on the other side of the world, was not exempt

from these strong winds of change and transition. A very noticeable change was the nation of Zimbabwe, formerly known as Rhodesia's transition into its long-awaited glorious future as it seemed at the time into majority rule with Robert Mugabe being elected as Prime Minister.

It was in March of that same year that I made my quiet but remarkable entrance into this material world. Ghana, the nation of my birth was going through its own transition. The political scene was marked with great instability with the threat of a looming coup d'état. Economically, the nation was in stagnation.

The shift from people patronizing nightclubs to churches and a rising number of Gospel musicians may have been an indication of the citizens' quest for hope in the midst of all the uncertainty.

As my mother tells the story of my birth, I arrived unexpectedly without the usual alert signs that accompany labor. I was delivered peacefully at home on an early Saturday morning at exactly 4 a.m weighing a whopping 11.5 pounds. Needless to say, I came in with a weight of presence...both literally and figuratively. By the time the doctor arrived, I was already comfortable in my new environment ready for a morning nap.

Aching for Home

"The ache for home lives in all of us, the safe place where we can go as we are and not be questioned." Maya Angelou

Perhaps being born at home and particularly during the onset of a great transitional decade must have something to do with my feeling of chronic "homesickness". For as long as I can remember, I have always had the desire to find "home". It is difficult for me to explain, but the imagery of a place of unconditional love, beauty, and acceptance where I would be given permission to grow, expand, to know and be known without fear or shame has always held a sacred space in my being. I am not sure when I exactly I uttered these prayers to the Lord asking Him to help me find "home" no matter the cost but I do know that at some point I did. Little did I know then that He was going to help me but not in the way that I had imagined it to look or feel like.

Growing up, I was a sheltered, quiet and shy little girl. A lot of my early memories have been blurred but I do remember that I having a deep longing for connection and a need or responsibility to please and be perfect because sadly, I had learned very early in life that love had to be earned. I also had a gift of empathy and a great concern for others. I could feel people's pain and always wished I could do something to help them. Sometimes, I would know about events or things about people before they actually happened. I did not know what to do with this gift so, over time, I learned to shut it off because the intensity of what I would feel or discern began to weigh on me emotionally.

At home, I pretty much did everything that was

expected of me. I helped my mother take care of the household which involved cooking, cleaning and helping take care of my brothers and sisters. This helped me gain a sense of responsibility at a very early age. I was blessed to have parents who empowered and encouraged me in whatever I did. My parents always told me that, I could be anything I desired to be in the world if I stuck to my education and I believed them!

I enjoyed school a lot and this obviously made my parents happy. English was one of my favorite subjects. My love for reading introduced me to the world at large. The stories awakened in me a profound sense of adventure. I wanted to travel and visit all the places I read about and experience the people and the cultures that were painted in the stories when I grew up.

One of my favorite places to go to as a young girl was Church. The smell of incense, the perfected order in which things were done and the sheer admiration I held for the nuns who sat on the front pew had me look forward to church services on Sundays. I always imagined myself dressed like them in their nicely pressed habits accessorized with a pearly rosary around my neck. I am pretty sure that is where my love for necklaces began!

Thankfully, one of the nuns finally noticed and befriended me. This friendship gave me a free pass to the convent. The rhythms of order, quiet peace and devotional discipline that I experienced at the convent made me want to become a nun when I grew up. Obviously, that did not happen. What the convent gave me was a little taste of what my heart knew and craved for "home" to be.

One other place that awakened in me the feeling of "home" was my maternal grandmother's home town Sogakope, an interesting little town located in the Volta region of Ghana. Going over to visit her with my family during school breaks was one of the highlights of my early childhood.

I remember fondly the great euphoria that would serenade my heart just before my parents' pick-up truck approached the bridge that would usher us into her village. Oh, the smell of the tiny stretch of the Volta River mixed with the aroma of the delectables sold by the agile and friendly hawkers by the roadside was such a beautiful welcome to me! The sound of their voices clamoring to be heard as they announced what they were selling as cars slowly passed by was sweet music to my ears. Sweet bread! Pure Water! Delicious shrimp, "abolo", "bofroot", etc. were some of the things that were yelled out. We would always stop to get some sweet bread. That made for a delicious gift for my grandmother's neighbors.

My grandmother's, delicious cooking and stories nourished my soul. The bond of friendship I had with the neighborhood kids grew every year. They equally looked forward with great excitement to the stories I would share with them from the city as much as I did to the stories they will share with me about the happenings in the village.

They didn't have much and so my parents always made sure we shared the little we had with them. The used clothing we brought them every year made for early Christmas presents. That experience of seeing first-hand what a long way a little act of kindness went sparked a desire for me to serve others with what I have when I grew up.

Tragedy Hits

"Hope is being able to see that there is light despite all of the darkness." Desmond Tutu

Most of my college days were wonderful! It was the first time I had moved to a different town by myself to do life and I was happy with this newfound freedom. My social circle widened as I added a collection of new friends to my old ones. Life was great! Everything looked promising and I felt I could take on the whole world after graduation. My idea of a promise of a successful life was almost within reach.

My life completely changed four months before I would complete college. My heart experienced a loss I was not ready or prepared for. A young man I was dating and was hoping to start a life with was tragically killed in a car crash.

The trauma split my heart into so many different pieces. The initial stage of shock, denial, and bargaining finally gave way to acceptance. I did not know at the time how to articulate or process the pain.

As I have thought over this tragic event over the last 15 years, I can see the fingerprint of God all over. As I can recall, a few months prior to the accident, I had re-dedicated my life to the Lord in a nearby spirit-filled church and started attending their service regularly.

This new "found faith" in God was the anchor that strengthened me during those dark times. I felt God's tangible presence and kindness more than any time in my life prior. This faith in God as a reliable anchor in times of need and uncertainty has been a part of my African heritage and I am so thankful for that seed to have been sown in me early in life.

After college, my family felt it would be therapeutic for me to change my environment so I went to visit my uncle and his family in England. After some months in England, I got an opportunity to move to America.

Something shifted in me as I set foot in America. My soul felt a warm embrace by both the land and the people. I felt there was enough room for me to grow and become not only in terms of the physical but figuratively it held the promise of a brand new beginning. I was delighted to start a new life in my new "home"

Discovering Anna

"It is only in solitude that I ever find my own core. " -Anne Morrow Lindbergh

The initial excitement I felt in America quickly gave way to feelings of disappointment, despair, and aloneness/solitude as I experienced broken dreams, closed doors and one set back after another. Being far away from family and close friends intensified these feelings. I realized that I had no road map or compass to navigate my new life. The sheltered life I had back in Ghana was a far cry from my new life in a land I had envisioned "milk and honey' flowing from right from the onset.

Little did I know at the time that all the closed doors were actually leading me to the right ones. God was answering the prayer that I had prayed as a little girl asking Him to help me find "Home". As my desperation to get an understanding of why every door that I attempted to knock on got slammed on at my face, my desire to know God as the only one who could understand and help me grew.

In this place of solitude, through various events and circumstances, I did find and experience God in a new way. As my knowledge of Him, through scripture and experience grew, my love and trust for Him did the same.

It was during this time that I realized and came into an understanding of my calling, design, purpose, and destiny. This was the "Home" I had been yearning for all my life! God is my "Home" and the more I discovered Him, the closer to home I experienced. I felt like I was experiencing a new birth or an awakening. The way I thought and looked at things began to change. For the first time in my life, who I thought I was, was gradually giving way to who God intended for me to be before the foundation of the universe. Every stronghold of self-protection, self-preservation, control, the need to please others and hence earn their love and the desire for success as the world defined it, began to gradually give way to a life of faith and trust in God even though I did not know or understand where this process will lead me to.

The Church, in America, became a strong and reliable support system for me. It served as a greenhouse for my transformation. In the safe company of fellow believers, the Lord began to awaken, nurture and steward the intuitive gift He had placed in me. As I grew in my giftings, I was given opportunities to help others discover and steward theirs also.

My love for studying the Bible continued to grow and I found a deep connection to biblical characters such as Abraham, Moses, Joseph, and Esther amongst others who were separated from their land of birth and transplanted to a new land where they met God and discovered the blueprint for their lives which served as a guide to serve the people of the land they were called out from.

During the middle of my transformation process, I discovered two things were happening to me simultaneously. I was being stripped of all the things that offended the promises of God for my life and also being clothed with a brand new identity of who I was in God. I was discovering Anna in a deeper way- as a life force, a conduit of love and as a quiet agent of change. I was piece by piece, evolving into a person, who was becoming free of the influence of thought processes shaped by cultures of community consciousness which inevitably lacked TRUTH.

As I continue to be on this process of discovering and evolving into my authentic self, I have learned to enjoy the process and give myself grace whenever I feel like I have missed the mark. I still occasionally have to watch the tendency of being "perfect" or the need to be understood and known for who I really am especially in unfamiliar spaces where I find myself to be for the most part. I am learning to give myself grace as I continue this journey. The past feelings of despair and aloneness have given way to feelings of hope and the knowledge that I am not alone. As, my spiritual wells, continue to be dug, I am discovering and experiencing fresh waters of effortless creative life flowing through me. As a result of this, many doors of favor and opportunity are being opened to me.

Bridging the Spiritual and Material Worlds

"You have to know your identity. It's the biggest thing in wanting to pursue creative dreams." Lauren Daigle

If you asked me who I am, my response to you today will be this "I am a Handmaiden of the Almighty God fashioned in the body of an African woman, called to build a bridge between Heaven (the world of the invisible) and Earth (the world of the visible).

This knowledge of who I am and becoming in both seasons of hiddenness and exposure gives me an understanding of my calling to the world, specifically to the continent of Africa, to serve and help my brothers and sisters to reclaim their identities and thus be free from the tyranny of religion and control. This work of restoration has already started and my heart is to partner with the Lord and the other change agents who are already doing great work or in the process.

A great transition is about to dawn on Africa, for both the people currently on the land and for those of African descent in the diaspora. The physical land is not going to be exempt from this change. After all, is said and done, the transition will lead to a glorious end. Just like many transitions that have happened in history, this one will not be exempt from the courage and great sacrifice that will be required by those on the forefront.

My part in this is embedded in a near future vision of creating a safe place or a "home", which will serve as a retreat center for spiritual and creative nourishment and thus a hub for deep spiritual and personal transformation that will cater to leaders and individuals around the world and also specifically for people of African descent in the diaspora. I envision this place to be on the banks of the Volta River in the Village where my grandmother once lived and the makeup of the center will in some ways reflect the quiet and spiritual reverence that I felt in the convent as a child. In this place, people will discover and experience the beauty and the heart of the Almighty God as a Father and a Friend and trust Him as the strength of their anchor as I have known and experienced Him to be.

Gratitude and Acknowledgements from the author:

Anna Owusu

Augustine and Wilhelmina

Joanna Vandyke Owusu

Dominic Owusu

Wilhelmina Essie Owusu

Kathleen Kennedy

About Anna Owusu

Anna Owusu is an Intercessor and a Creative Visionary. With a Bachelors in social work from the University of Ghana and a Master's in Theology from Life Christian University, she has more than a decade of experience in church leadership. Anna has ministered to hundreds of people from different church denominations, generational, spiritual and racial backgrounds. She believes in the compelling power of the Love of God expressed through Gentleness, Kindness, and Compassion as the catalyst for all Healing and Transformation.

Anna is a Certified Aromatherapist where she uses essential oils (natural plant extracts) to help people heal holistically. She is also the visionary behind Holistic Locs by Anna, a natural hair venture where her mission is to help people of color walk in their uniqueness and identity through the freedom of expressing their beauty through their natural hair. She also makes organic hair care and skin care products. www.holisticlocsbyanna.com

Her vision is to establish a Retreat and Healing Center in Ghana where she was born and raised. This will serve as a safe haven of Spiritual and Creative Nourishment for pioneers and leaders from all over the world. www.wellsoftransformationnetwork.com

Kathy Clark

"She has fire in her soul and grace in her heart." - Unknown

Uniquely Designed

By: Kathy Clark

I had life all wrong – all wrong. No, wait, my life was all wrong. At half of a century of life, I believe I am closest to who I was intended to be.

I don't believe in brokenness as a form of identity. I believe it's a form of de-identification. As we are born, we are born with a beautiful and unique blueprint that is lovingly and thoughtfully designed by God. When you think of a child who looks up to the world full of pure joy with any task…that is the pure essence of who we truly are.

Over the years, who we are begins to break down. As we lose sight of ourselves with good intentions of giving to others, we begin to break small pieces of ourselves away to make room for who we thought they wanted us to be. It seems so innocuous and innocent at the time. But one day – one moment, we wake up realizing we don't know who we are anymore. We are unhappy, discontent and probably even depressed.

My first thirty-five years of life was a slow degradation of the precious soul I was given. The value and joy I had were so broken which began at a very early age. I was born with gifts that were not readily accepted and cherished. To refer to the Clifton StrengthsFinder, my top five strengths are Woo (Winning Others Over), Connectedness, Input, Compassion, and Positivity. Needless to say, these are mostly all involving relational skills. Put me in a home that was difficult to connect on a deep level and you can see why I was craving connection. As I say, I was born to love and be free. Sometimes I think I was born a gypsy because I craved adventure with a ton of courage to boot.

For instance, as a toddler, one Sunday morning, the house must have been quiet because I have never really been crazy about quiet spaces for too long. I pushed the ottoman to the door to undo the chain on the door while I was wearing my yellow Winnie the Pooh footie pajamas. I took my tricycle out and exited the house. It must have been very quiet because I cannot imagine how I escaped without my family waking up. In what appears to be a site for sore eyes to an extrovert, I saw people entering into a church. Remember the courage part? Well, I took my trusty tricycle and rode up the aisle of the church. Needless to say, some churchgoer brought me home.

As an empath, I craved peace, love, and connection, and it was so hard to find at home. Through no fault of anyone's in a home where disconnection seemed to be the norm, I began learning that disconnecting from me was necessary to offset the disappointment of needs that were going unmet. It was at this time I subconsciously began to abandon myself for the shallow gift of approval, acceptance, and company. The secrets at this point began compounding for sanity's sake. The more I denied my true self, the weaker I became. Hollowed and cracked – the miracle I found to glue myself back together was alcohol. Immediately following the first sip, the dopamine quickly filled my gaps and glued me back to me…for a bit.

Every choice I made was anchored externally. I was devoid and detached from emotions for years. I had my Mother convinced as well that "nothing ever phased me." I remember when I wanted to cry, the tear that would gently approach the open air was snatched back so quickly as to keep the proof that I cared away from the world. My necessary and total love affair with alcohol lasted until I was 35 and spiritually dead. I remember how I felt upon the decision to quit drinking. I was facing the possibility that I would never have fun again because alcohol lied that I could only have fun without it. Day-by-day, I made the choice to choose emotional sobriety over drinking. It was a choice that worked for the years to come. I couldn't have done many of the things I accomplished without being a quitter. Even the whisper of my heart saying, "I want to go to nursing school."

Through a succession of following the breadcrumbs of life, in 2010, I discovered that there was a community college not too far away that had the only evening nursing program for a two-year degree. I began the pre-requisites and on my first attempt to apply in 2012, I was accepted. I was stunned and ecstatic and began nursing school in January 2013. This year also proved to be one of my happiest years. I met my boyfriend at the time, was riding motorcycles and was probably the most confident I had been in my life. It was the beginning of the end for me and I didn't know it at the time. The following year proved to be one of the most challenging years I have faced because the anchors I had methodically placed around me were about to disappear completely.

My third semester of nursing school was the spring of 2014. It was challenging. My boyfriend lost his job as we were living together and school had never really been easy for me having graduated high school at the top 90% of my high school. I almost didn't graduate high school. At the end of the semester for nursing school...I had missed passing by 0.70 points. Right at this time, my boyfriend accepted a job in Connecticut and I surrendered that I would give up my schooling and move there with him. We had a trip planned to look for houses to rent and found a home to rent that included our six dogs which was a miracle in itself. Two hours after signing the lease on the house, I got a call from the nursing school. The message was "we've decided to recalculate the grades, would you like to come back and finish out your fourth semester of nursing school." I was stunned to say the least with a resounding "yes!" So, we had a change of plans. I would stay in Houston until I finished nursing school and then would relocate.

Then another whisper entered my heart. This was a whisper I had been ignoring for a bit. As much as I loved my boyfriend, I couldn't help the fact that our lifestyles were destined to tear us apart. Even as he moved up to Connecticut with a new job, the disconnection became more evident and my sobriety would either have to take a back seat or I would have had to work harder at ignoring that there was more than casual drinking occurring. You see, when you love someone, I couldn't keep living a lie knowing that I couldn't or wouldn't want to change him and we decided to end it which promptly left me moving out of his home. A friend allowed me to stay with her. I was so grateful for this and had the majority of my dogs in boarding and lived out of a couple of suitcases while I slept on her sofa looking for a home that would allow me to rent with my five dogs.

One day, my friend came inside and said the house across the street was having a garage sale and since I had really nothing from moving out, I went over and looked. I really didn't see anything and went back inside. My friend came back inside a second time saying that the people having the garage sale were moving to Reno and I might be able to rent the house. I was in disbelief that it could happen but decided to go over there anyway and inquire about it. In the questioning, the tenants said they were renting from their friend and they were not paying much in rent. I wound up speaking with the owner of the property, provided her references for my dogs from my prior landlord and met her for coffee. Although she was surprised at the number of dogs I had, she agreed to rent the property to me for the said price because I had 'good energy.' At this time, I was so grateful. I saw the house and it was exactly what I needed.

Throughout the time I was staying with my friend, I had neck pain that became acutely painful quickly. I couldn't lift a gallon of milk and had numbness and pain going down to my fingers. The diagnosis was that I had herniations in two of my cervical discs. Two physicians recommended surgery and I was starting my fourth and final semester of my nursing degree. If I had surgery, I would have to wait to finish and there was no way I was going to ruin the chance God had given me to finish. Right at this time, is when I also found out that my Step-Dad who walked me down the aisle when I got married passed away five months prior. No one had notified me of his passing and I was devastated. It shouldn't have been such a shock because we had been estranged since shortly after my Mom's passing, but this on top of everything else brought me to a new level of surrender and grief. At this point, I seemingly felt I had lost everything…my boyfriend, Step-Dad, a home, belongings. The only things I had intact at this point were my dogs which were still in boarding with the exception of one.

As I went through my last semester of nursing school, I successfully avoided surgery by getting cortisone injections and dry deep needling done by a chiropractor. This seemed to remedy the severe symptoms and had a 30% improvement in pain by the third week of treatment. The light was shining at the end of the tunnel with nursing school. I hunkered down studying regularly with a friend and it seemed to be working. As I approached graduation, I bought the scrubs with the intention of graduating. I volunteered to put my name in the hat to be elected for doing a speech at graduation and did anything I could to show how eager I was to cross the finish line.

As December approached and the elections were made for students who were going to be providing speeches at graduation, I was voted in by my peers.

Graduation night was one of the happiest days in my life. I was beaming. My family had come into town for it and I was so blessed. I was surrounded by the most amazing classmates anyone could have and as we were sitting there listening to the names being called out for awards, I heard "....Kathy Clark."

I literally looked around for another Kathy Clark and then realized that I was awarded the Clinical Simulation Award. I was thinking...wait a minute, you know I failed, right? You surely called out the wrong student...and sure enough, there was the award with my name on it. All of this just doesn't happen without purpose.

Two months after graduation, I passed my NCLEX and received my nursing license. It was complete. I began to relax and as I rested into myself, I had nothing but me and my accomplishments left. This wasn't a bad thing and in fact, it was the best thing that could have happened. It was at this point that I realized all of those labels I affixed to myself as a child and growing up became negated. If you've ever had an existential or spiritual crisis, you'll know what I mean when I say I was naked with me and for me for the first time in my life. I remember sitting in my bed, numb head to toe with the words coming out of my mouth, "this is it. This is all there is." I remember reading at some point during this time, "When I seek God, I find me. When I seek within, I find God." I wasn't necessarily searching for God, but because I was devoid of all labels and lies about me I was faced with the undeniable truth of me. It was at this time, that I understood that this was the time that I had for self-discovery. This is the part that I began to anchor into my own strength and not the strength of outside influences, things or people.

On Friday, February 20, 2015, I was sitting in my bed, numb. It was the closest that I have ever felt to me and to God. These words spilled out of me effortlessly...

"I offer to you my struggle, I offer to you my fight. I am nothing and yet I am everything. It is by showing you my vulnerabilities is how I gain my strength and freedom. By embracing my brokenness I have glued myself into wholeness. The wholeness comes from my willingness and ability to love that thing I hated within me and God offered me the tools and the path from which to learn. It is with my centeredness that my intuition is confirmed because there is a feeling of peace when I act on guidance from God. That alignment of my intuitive spirit and God's direction provides the centeredness ."

I grieved for eight straight months, crying nearly every day. I wasn't grieving the things I lost, I was grieving who I had abandoned for nearly a half-century. I found a group of women that let me just be. That was the best gift I could have gotten at that point. No one told me I was bad or to pull my pants up or suck it up. They just let me be.

At this point, again, brokenness is nothing but the pieces we shave off of ourselves to become the person we need to be in order to make us right with them. I had way too many years of doing that. With my family, ex-husband, boyfriend, friends and even with myself! How empty my vessel became each time I threw the anchor overboard trying to connect with anything that would prove me to be worthy, lovable, acceptable and likable outside of myself.

I would like to say that at this point my life got easier. It did in some ways and didn't in others. What made it worthwhile was that I had enough of myself to anchor into so those things that moved off my plate were intended to free me of bonds that were keeping me embracing my full self. Would I do it over again? The answer would be, yes. I've come to know and love myself in a way I have never loved me before. I'm not worth discounting for anything or anyone. No one is. We are uniquely designed for a purpose with gifts. We are meant to use them, all of them. When we do that, we are free.

Gratitude and Acknowledgements from the author:

<u>Kathy Clark</u>
Amy and Shaw Bodden
Keith and Melissa Bodden
Rilla Askew
Shari Hendricks
Gail Spann
Kathy Bartlett
Angela LaMonte
Jolene Dupnick
Terry Westfahl
Peggy Aalund
Karla Goolsby
Kelly Cole
Amy Robinson
Terri Cates
Patti Stone
Erin Smith
Angela McKinney
Cathy Arlinghaus
Kim LaMontagne
Deborah Trejo
Barbara Williams Webb
Gary De Rodriguez
Donna Fuller

THE STRENGTH OF OUR ANCHORS

Annie Dieu

Cody and Mirhonda Field

Monica Vils-Brawner

Maud Lipscomb

Patsy Futral

Lloyd and Josie Edgecombe

Mom and Dad

Dawn Bornheimer

Kim Kaase

Dawn Hammatt

About Kathy Clark

Kathy Clark, BSN, RN, is a speaker, scholar, writer, executive, and passionate community volunteer. Kathy is a member of the American Nurses Association National Alliance on Mental Illness and hone her skills as a Registered Nurse by traveling to third world countries to work with medical aid mission teams. Presently, her thirst for knowledge is quenched by her studies toward a Master of Science in Leadership and Organizational Development with a concentration in Executive Coaching, and by her intentional openness to finding wisdom in the everyday. A self-described empath and extrovert, Kathy has learned to make room for serendipity by listening to the small voice, the intuition that tells her to strike up a conversation with an unlikely stranger. In these encounters the ordinary becomes extraordinary and her circuitous path to professional, personal and scholarly fulfillment is enriched.

With her coaching certification through the International Coaching Federation, Kathy has eagerly begun her endeavor of personal and professional development with IBA Coaching (www.ibacoaching.com), Imagine Believe Achieve.

A native of New Orleans, Kathy currently resides in the Houston area where animal lovers know her through her volunteer efforts, rescuing and fostering abandoned pets and housing as many as six, four-legged dependents at once.

Tina Paulus-Krause

"Be the change you wish to see in the world." Mahatma Gandhi

The Anchor is YOU!

By: Tina Paulus-Krause

I've been an overachiever my whole life: a workaholic always looking for what was next. I used to wear "busy" on my forehead as if it were some kind of a badge of honor. I had one hell of a "to do" list and I loved checking the items off. Each check gave me this sense of accomplishment. Despite checking off item after item, my list never shrank. I was on this hamster wheel going around and around and that wheel only sped up instead of slowing down. In my drive to succeed, I became consumed by worry; always taking care of everyone else and everything else before myself. I didn't see it at the time, but it came with a heavy price. Today, I realize all those lists and the constant need to schedule myself to the ultimate limit was a means of distraction; a way to avoid other issues in my life. Ouch. It's hard to own what you own.

As the days, weeks, months, and years passed, I barely noticed life passing by, so caught up in the hustle and bustle of life. This is how a typical day might look. The alarm goes off, I hit snooze a few times, so that I run out of time to work-out. When I get up, I shower, get the kids up, and make sure they are ready: feed them breakfast (though I don't eat myself), get their things ready for the day, and speed out of the house into the car. A mile down the road, realize something (or someone) had been forgotten, so drive back, grab basketball shoes, hop back in the car to drop off at multiple schools, and then frantically drive to the office just in time for an 8 AM meeting.

Once I get to work, fly through a series of back-to-back meetings that necessitate skipping lunch. By the time 5 o'clock rolls around, I run out the door (already running late) to pick up the kids from school, drive through to get them dinner before taking them to their sports practices and games, academic activities, etc. and hurry them home afterward. Then we rush through ~~their~~ homework, get them ready for bed, and tuck them in. After that, there's laundry to start and fold, dishes to wash from earlier in the day, meals to prep for tomorrow, e-mails (both personal and professional) to answer. Finally at around 1 AM, I crash, only to wake up a few hours later to reach out and hit the snooze button and repeat the same day. Do you feel me?

When we live our life like this, in constant chaos and turmoil, it's impossible to find clarity or depth. So, we live on the surface and survive. It's hard to find time to take care of ourselves so that in moments that matter, we aren't able to show up in the way we need to or as the best version of who we truly are, affecting both personal and professional success.

We live to make everything on the outside work. Because we aren't taking care of ourselves, we become more and more unhealthy. We burn out. I was buried under emotions - ready to explode at any minute. This is how I was living my life. Then one day, I got a phone call that changed everything. In that moment, all of the noise and chaos went away.

It was a Sunday morning around 10 AM. When she spoke those words "Something really bad happened last night," it was as if the whole universe stopped. I felt alone and scared. How was I ever going to help her through this? I didn't have a plan for this and I always had a plan. I could fix anything, but not this. Up until that moment, I believed that I was a positive person, even when things got difficult. But this was different: my world went dark. I literally felt the darkness cover my life the moment that call came in. It was the first time in my life that I literally shut my life down. I hit PAUSE. In a moment of clarity, I just hit pause. Nothing else mattered.

I knew in that second, this was a moment I could not miss. I didn't know what or why, but I knew in my soul that it was a moment that mattered. It felt different. My internal voice was screaming that she deserved my complete focus in that moment. Looking back, I was trying to make up for the thousand other times I didn't give her my focus. The times I missed basketball games because of work or skipped bedtime rituals to spend time on my laptop – those moments came crashing into my mind. I knew I had to be fully and wholly present.

That Sunday morning, she crashed into my arms and I cradled her - a shattered mess. She was reeling from the actions of her boyfriend the night before. He turned out to be a bad person. And, as the next few days unraveled, I learned about her severe addiction to drugs and alcohol. I held her in my arms as she hit her rock bottom. Her anchor had been stuck in a very dark place for too long.

As I sat there, a part of me went into shock and became overwhelmed with guilt – the guilt of a mother who felt she'd failed her child. Another part felt this surge of warmth and somehow, I knew I was being given a chance to do things different. My history with my children is that of enablement and this was my chance to show up differently than I had in the past. With a new mindset I made a decision to try something new. In that moment, I knew I had work to do in order to change the trajectory of not only her life, but mine as well.

We spent the week locked up in the house. Lots of crying and laughing, talking and connecting deeply. Research. We dug in. Nothing else mattered. I have a strong history of enabling and I wanted so bad to "fix" it. To say what needed to be done and then probably do it all. Instead of fixing it, like I had too many times before, I stood as strong support as she worked through her past and decided the fate of her future. As she made decisions about what came next, I was by her side empowering her to dig deep, stay centered, and find clarity. This was her journey, not mine.

I will never forget the day a week later when I drove her to the airport with a one-way ticket. I didn't know what she was entering into. She had decided to try a 30-day rehab program. At that moment, I didn't have the answers when I'd always had the answers in the past. At least I thought I did. As I watched her go up the escalator to her gate, I surrendered and handed it all over to God. And I prayed. HARD. And I trusted the professionals at that rehab facility with her life. It was the longest 30 days of my life, and hers.

They say in every struggle, there is a lesson. This was a hard one for me. I hadn't always shown up like I needed to for those that depended on me the most. I missed signs people closest to me were in trouble. As I look back, the signs were there for years and I missed them because I was on this hamster wheel - trying to do all and be it all for everyone. The tough lesson I learned was to get clear, slow down, and be present. Because I was so scattered, I had no clarity, no priority, and I was just living and existing day to day with no anchor to hold me in one place. My lesson was that my job wasn't to fix, my job was to be her anchor in those moments that mattered. To stand strong at her side as she fixed it.

Leading in today's environment requires a different skill set with a new set of tools centered on mindful leadership and consciousness. It starts with the ability to manage ourselves in this newly connected and constantly changing world. It requires the discipline to manage the hamster wheel from a place of clarity. When you have clarity of your true intentions, you won't miss the moments that matter.

How do you show up? For yourself? Your team? Your clients? How do you show up for your family and friends? In good times, showing up with a positive attitude and good, solid decision-making is easy. In times of conflict, chaos, or tragedy – the moments that truly matter – how do you manage your reactions and choices? Choosing how to show up in these moments paves the path through your life: your career successes, your relationships with your family, and the connections you form with friends.

I was guilty of standing before the mirror in the morning and thinking about my day to come and saying horrible things to myself. Things I'd never say to anyone else. Never. I wasn't showing up for myself, so how could I possibly show up and lead others? Yet I had colleagues and clients depending on me to help grow their businesses. And, family who I was letting down because when I was communicating with them, I was stressed and angry.

Showing up is about conscious choice and discipline has to be a part of the equation. How one shows up during conflict will make the difference between a good leader and a great leader.

There is power in the ability to pause before reacting. In the moment, we often let emotions lead how we react and the result is less than ideal. The time to pause is in that moment immediately following a situation and before responding. By choosing to train our brains to manage that pause and think about our responses, we create more balanced and productive outcomes that strengthen relationships instead of allowing our immediate emotional responses to leave a path of destruction.

Knowing that, how do we find time to keep our minds in check? Can you feel your world spinning out of control? Are you bombarded by words, data, and information coming at you through verbal, written, and electronic media? Do you feel the need to check in on the news of the world, answer emails, respond to messages sent and photos posted on social media, keep up with new series online and on the TV, etc., etc., etc? Do you feel like even though our world is more connected than ever, our lives just keep getting busier and busier instead of better and better?

And it's not just noisy outside. It's plenty noisy inside of you as well! Did you know on average we have

70,000 thoughts per day? Here's a shocking fact: 80% of those daily thoughts are negative. That's 56,000 negative thoughts per day. How scary is that?! How do we combat all of these inputs and the mass of negativity to stay positive and productive? Intention.

Leading from the inside out means consistently and intentionally practicing the pause in everything you do. The pause is so powerful! Learning to pause makes it possible to differentiate yourself from others; your reaction is your choice. Bottom line. As a leader, it all starts with you. Emotions lead us to react in the moment. I am inviting you to pause. Pause and respond from a place of empathy and caring. If you can't lead yourself in these times, how can you possibly lead others?

How you lead yourself sets the stage for every other relationship you have, both personally and professionally, regardless of income, title or rank. It also sets the stage for the level of success you are willing and allowing yourself to have. It is difficult to identify your dreams and work to reach them when you are living in negative, thinking you've got it and know it all. If this is you, you don't got it. You don't know it all. No one does. We all have room to grow.

Believing in self is the key. Loving yourself anchors you to your true authentic essence and allows you to become who you are meant to be.

After 22 years at a large corporation, I took the leap and now dedicate my future to helping others get unstuck. I started a company, True You, LLC Coaching and Consulting dedicated to leadership development: leadership of self and others. I help people, teams, and organizations grow their leadership skills so they can live their best life, ignite results and leave a lasting leadership legacy.

I found the key. The anchor was me. The stronger I get in loving and believing in myself, the more I am anchored in love and connectedness back to myself as the source. I am the creator of my life. You are the creator of your life. The amazing fact is that it doesn't matter how old you are, what your body type is, the emotional baggage you carry with you, or your past experiences. Right now, right here, you can decide. You can choose to show up different. You can choose to get clear on who you want to be, and then build your life around becoming that person. Day by day, step by step. It's a choice. You can continue to enable the life that is unhappy and maybe toxic, or empower a life of joy and fulfillment. Once you make the choice, there are many resources for you to help you succeed.

We all get stuck. In those moments, it's easy to feel alone. You are not alone. There is a full life waiting to be lived. A life waiting for you to decide it's time to let go and commit. You are the anchor of your life. You can use that anchor to keep you in a life you don't love OR you can use the anchor to find your center and rise up and create the life you dream of living.

Take your power back. Create your best life! What are you waiting for? The anchor is YOU!

Final thoughts from the author:

I want to acknowledge those who stood by my side and held me high as I was trying to figure out how to hold myself high. Thank you. I am forever grateful. XO

I deeply acknowledge my loving husband and beautiful kids for giving me a purpose to always strive to be a better me. You are my north star and my reason why.

In love, light and leadership,

Tina

Gratitude and Acknowledgements from the author:

Tina Paulus - Krause

Al Krause

Courtney Paulus

Tanner Paulus

Alex Krause

Aubrie Krause

Adam Krause and Marie Brenner

Jean and Dennis Kiner

Dusty and Kristin Kiner

Denny and Nikki Kiner

About Tina Paulus-Krause

Tina is a captivating speaker, a Huffington Post blogger, and the Co-Host of a local access TV show called Our Focus is You. After 22 years in corporate, Tina took the leap and founded a leadership development company dedicated to helping leaders become stronger, healthier, evolved leaders. Her passion is in transformational coaching and helping people become the best leader of themselves and others they can be.

After a complete transformation of her own, Tina learned how powerfully leveraging the right tools combined with a trusting community, can reprogram long-held beliefs, change long-held habits and create sustainable results. Tina has made it her mission to help leaders and teams dig deep and learn to empower themselves to reach their fullest potential.

Our world has and is dramatically changing and so must how we develop as leaders. New skill sets are needed as we rapidly move into the future of work. Tina's life experience and background of 22 years in business, provide a perfectly unique and well-rounded framework where she can speak and coach from a place of true authenticity helping others create sustainable change.

Tina is married to Al and together they have five adult children and a puppy named Rocki

Dawn M. Bornheimer

Visionary Author

"When you come out of the storm, you won't be the same person who walked in. That's what this storm's all about. " -Haruki Murakami

About Dawn Bornheimer

Dawn Marie Bornheimer is an industry leader with a unique combination of interpersonal, business, and strategic skills. Her 17 years of professional experience have taken her from classroom teacher to world-class sales and marketing executive.

A contributing author and frequent speaker on the topic of leadership, Dawn strives to help support young girls and women to find their voice. She works closely with emerging leaders to help them lead with their WHY and intention as they step into the next best version of themselves. She believes that through mentoring and being mentored, we all play an essential role in our individual and collective success.

www.dawninspires.com

Gratitude and Acknowledgements from the author:

<u>Dawn Marie Bornheimer</u>

Charles Banks

Barbara Banks

My Loving Family

My Newport Friends

Lisa Sharkey

The Ulman Foundation

My P2P Family

Key West Friends for Life

Truth Arising Spirit Gang

Bliss Sisters

YES to You Mastermind

52795927R00081

Made in the USA
Columbia, SC
12 March 2019